# GLOBETROTTER™

## Travel Guide

# BOTSWANA

## Alan Brough

NEW
HOLLAND

NEW
HOLLAND

***  Highly recommended
 **  Recommended
  *  See if you can

Seventh edition published in 2013
by New Holland (Publishers) Ltd
London • Cape Town • Sydney • Auckland
10 9 8 7 6 5 4 3 2 1
website: www.newhollandpublishers.com

Garfield House, 86 Edgware Road,
London W2 2EA, United Kingdom

Wembley Square, First Floor, Solan Road,
Gardens, Cape Town 8001, South Africa

Unit 1, 66 Gibbes Street, Chatswood,
NSW 2067, Australia

218 Lake Road, Northcote,
Auckland, New Zealand

Distributed in the USA by
The Globe Pequot Press, Connecticut

ISBN 978 1 78009 430 4

**Keep us Current**
Information in travel guides is apt to change, which is why
we regularly update our guides. We'd be grateful to receive
feedback if you've noted something we should include in
our updates. If you have new information, please share it
with us by writing to the Publishing Manager, Globetrotter,
at the office nearest to you (addresses on this page). The
most significant contribution to each new edition will
receive a free copy of the updated guide.

This guidebook has been written by independent authors and
updaters. The information therein represents their impartial
opinion, and neither they nor the publishers accept payment
in return for including in the book or writing more favourable

reviews of any of the establishments. Whilst every effort has
been made to ensure that this guidebook is as accurate and
up to date as possible, please be aware that the facts quoted
are subject to change, particularly the price of food, transport
and accommodation. The Publisher accepts no responsibility
or liability for any loss, injury or inconvenience incurred by
readers or travellers using this guide.

**Publishing Manager:** Thea Grobbelaar
**DTP Cartographic Manager:** Genené Hart
**Editors:** Thea Grobbelaar, Carla Zietsman, Nicky Steenkamp,
Melany Porter, Laurence Lemmon-Warde, Anouska Good
**Cartographers:** Nicole Bannister, Reneé Spocter, Inga
Ndibongo, Genené Hart, Marisa Roman, John Hall, Éloïse
Moss
**Design and DTP:** Nicole Bannister, Laurence Lemmon-
Warde, Sonya Cupido
**Compiler/Verifier:** Elaine Fick
Reproduction by Hirt & Carter (Pty) Ltd, Cape Town.
Printed and bound by Craft Print International Ltd, Singapore.

**Acknowledgments:** The author would like to express his
appreciation to the various travel and safari operators and
establishments, especially the management and staff of
Okavango Wilderness Safaris whose generous support has
greatly enhanced the content of this book. Their standard
of professional conduct and environmental concern in
ensuring the long-term sustainable development of
Botswana's outstanding tourist attractions for all its visitors
are exemplary.

**Photographic Credits:**
**Daryl Balfour,** title page, pages 8–10, 12, 18, 19, 22, 23, 25,
28, 29, 30, 33, 35, 37, 38, 52, 59, 60, 62, 64, 66, 69–72,
78, 82, 85, 86, 88, 91, 92 (bottom), 93–102, 106, 112, 113,
116, 117 (top), 119; **Daryl and Sharna Balfour/IOA,** 58;
**Michael Brett,** pages 7, 44, 47–49, 75, 81, 84; **Alan Brough:**
page 39; **Cape Archives** (Depot), pages 15, 16; **Colour
Library/IOA,** page 6; **Roger de la Harpe/IOA,** page 103 (top
and bottom); **Nigel J Dennis/IOA,** 56; **Bev Flinn,** page 50;
**Leonard Hoffman/IOA,** pages 13, 73; **Illustrative Options,**
pages 11, 14, 20, 21, 24, 26, 40, 55, 57, 61, 63, 74, 83, 92
(top), 110, 111, 114, 115, 118; **Ian Michler/IOA,** 4; **Ulf
Nermark/Activepic,** 34; **Peter Pickford/IOA,** pages 27, 41;
**Travel Pictures Ltd.,** cover.
[IOA = Images of Africa]

**Cover:** *Mokoro trip on the Okavango Delta.*
**Title page:** *A herd of buffalo (*Syncerus caffer*) gallop
across shallow lagoons in the Okavango Delta.*

# CONTENTS

# 1
# Introducing Botswana

With its unspoiled wildernesses and promise of adventure, Botswana is one of the last remaining safari destinations in Africa where you can still experience nature as the early explorers did.

This magnificent country boasts a treasure trove of options for the tourist, from the famous **Okavango Delta** wetlands to the incredible **Makgadikgadi salt pans**, from grass plains of migrating zebra to the stark openness of the **Kalahari** and the huge herds of elephant in **Chobe**.

Botswana is one of the world's most thinly populated countries with just 3.5 people per km² (6 per sq mile), and at independence in 1966 it was also one of the poorest. However, since then there has been remarkable growth in all sectors of the economy, including tourism, conservation and wildlife management.

With almost 20% of the country protected as national park or wildlife management area, Botswana has made a real commitment to conservation, and many of its people have now begun to appreciate the value of managed conservation areas. The Nata Sanctuary was one of the first examples of how the local population can financially benefit from the administration of their own wildlife areas. Although, unlike most other African countries, this trend has been evident in Botswana since the early 1960s, when the Batawana people agreed that their traditional hunting grounds in the Okavango should be protected. This act was hailed as a landmark in African tribal history and the area was named the Moremi Game Reserve after the late Chief Moremi III.

## TOP ATTRACTIONS

\*\*\* **The Okavango:** mokoro trails, game viewing, walking safaris, fishing.
\*\*\* **The Chobe:** elephant, fishing, birding and game viewing.
\*\*\* **The Makgadikgadi:** exploring, driving, camping, flamingoes.
\*\* **The Kalahari:** lions, gemsbok, vast unspoiled landscapes.
\*\* **Tuli:** night drives, walking safaris, leopard, hyena, elephant.

◀ *Opposite: A baobab tree mirrored in the waters of the Okavango.*

## THE LAND

Located in the centre of southern Africa and covering an area of 581,730km² (224,548 sq miles), Botswana is a landlocked country, just slightly smaller than the U.S. state of Texas. Namibia lies to the west and north of the country with the thin Caprivi Strip which runs along the top of Botswana. While to the south lies South Africa and to the east there is Zimbabwe. In the northeast for just 700m (765yd) Botswana and Zambia meet along the world's shortest international boundary.

Extending through nine degrees of latitude, two thirds of the country lies within the **tropics**, but unlike most 'tropical' countries, Botswana is dry and prone to drought. The vast **Kalahari Desert**, the largest continuous stretch of sand in the world, covers 84% of Botswana, extending from the Orange River in South Africa right up to the equator in Gabon.

When the supercontinent of Gondwana started breaking up about 200 million years ago, three basins were formed through the middle of central and southern Africa. The Kalahari Basin was the last of these, and it is now almost completely full of wind-blown Aeolian sand, levelling the country to an average height of 950m (3117ft) above sea level.

Granite gneiss rocks formed the base of this original basin, which is now covered by up to 200m (656ft) of sand, but along the borders of the country, particularly around Francistown and in the southern Barolong area, fragments of these ancient rocks – possibly the oldest rocks in the world at more than 3.5 billion years of age – can still be found. Overlaying this deeply buried foundation stone is a matrix of Karoo deposits made up of sandstone, basalt lavas, shales and thin seams of coal, all about 300 million years old.

## FACTS AND FIGURES

**Total size** – 581,730km² (224,548 sq miles).
**World's largest inland delta** – Okavango, covering approximately 15,000km² (5790 sq miles).
**World's largest salt pans** – Makgadikgadi pans complex covering approximately 12,000km² (4632 sq miles).
**World's shortest border** – Botswana's border with Zambia is only 700m (765yd) long.
**Neighbours** – bordered by Namibia, South Africa, Zambia and Zimbabwe.
**Driest country** – there is only one perennial river, the Okavango, that flows into Botswana and none flow out of the country.
**Highest point** – Otse Hill, 1489m (4885ft) above sea level.

One of Botswana's more recent – and more fortunate – geological events was the eruption of several **kimberlitic volcanic pipes** which punched through the earth's crust some 80 million years ago. Under the right temperature and pressure conditions the carbon contained in some of these lavas changed over a long period of time into the **diamonds** which today fuel Botswana's economic development.

▲ *Above: A blowing sandstorm dusts down the Kalahari just before the summer rains break.*
◄ *Opposite: The characteristic red dunes of the Kgalagadi Transfrontier Park.*

While Botswana is often depicted as being a flat featureless semidesert, there is much wonder and variation to be found in this vast land. One of the greatest paradoxes this arid sandveld encompasses is the lush, verdant jewel of the **Okavango Delta** formed as the wide, fast-flowing Okavango River spills out across a massive area of sand where it eventually soaks away, drying up in its futile search for the sea.

Other remarkable features punctuating Botswana's terrain include the immense **Makgadikgadi pans**, whose salt-cracked surface marks the death bed of the great Lake Makgadikgadi. Along the eastern edge of the country, the landscape has more variety with hills and *kopjes* (rocky mounds), while in the far west and southwest, deep in the Kalahari, the terrain is completely flat and arid.

## Climate

As is typical of deserts far from the moderating influence of the sea, and as the country extends over nine degrees of latitude, there is considerable variation in the seasons and climatic conditions in Botswana.

| COMPARATIVE CLIMATE CHART | GABORONE | | | | FRANCISTOWN | | | | MAUN | | | |
|---|---|---|---|---|---|---|---|---|---|---|---|---|
| | SUM | AUT | WIN | SPR | SUM | AUT | WIN | SPR | SUM | AUT | WIN | SPR |
| | JAN | APR | JULY | OCT | JAN | APR | JULY | OCT | JAN | APR | JULY | OCT |
| MIN TEMP. °C | 20 | 13 | 4 | 16 | 19 | 14 | 5 | 16 | 20 | 16 | 7 | 19 |
| MAX TEMP. °C | 33 | 27 | 23 | 31 | 31 | 28 | 23 | 31 | 33 | 32 | 26 | 36 |
| MIN TEMP. °F | 68 | 55 | 39 | 61 | 66 | 57 | 41 | 61 | 68 | 61 | 45 | 66 |
| MAX TEMP. °F | 91 | 81 | 73 | 88 | 88 | 82 | 73 | 88 | 91 | 90 | 79 | 97 |
| RAINFALL mm | 104 | 50 | 4 | 46 | 99 | 28 | 0 | 31 | 112 | 27 | 0 | 19 |
| RAINFALL in | 4.1 | 2 | 0.2 | 1.8 | 3.9 | 1.1 | 0 | 1.2 | 4.4 | 1.1 | 0 | 0.7 |

▶ *Opposite: The golden grasslands of the Central Kalahari Game Reserve stretch away as far as the eye can see.*
▼ *Below: The tranquil waters of the Chobe River beautifully reflect the dying embers of the setting sun.*

There are generally only two seasons: summer, which lasts from October to April; and winter which is slightly shorter, from May to September. The vast majority of rain falls between December and February, although even during this period there can be long dry spells when temperatures can soar to over 40°C (104°F). In winter the night temperatures can plummet to below freezing. But at any time of year, be it midwinter or midsummer, visitors can generally count on sunny clear blue skies with very few consistently cloudy days.

Rainfall is often in the form of short, sharp thunderstorms followed by sunshine, which, while good for tourists, is detrimental to farmers as it causes much of the precipitation to evaporate before it can soak into the soil. The quantity and reliability of rainfall decreases from the northeast of the country, where 600mm (24in) can be expected with a variability of 30%, to the southwest, where an average annual rainfall of only 200mm (8in) can have a seasonal variation of up to 80%.

### Rivers and Mountains

Apart from the **Okavango River** there is no other perennial water supply flowing into, or out of, Botswana. Only the **Chobe River** in the extreme north, which separates Botswana from Namibia's Caprivi Strip flows all year round. For this reason, water is one of Botswana's most precious commodities and there is grave concern about its availability for a growing population in the near future.

The Chobe, Okavango and Zambezi rivers all have their source in the rain-drenched eastern Angolan highlands, where there is an average annual rainfall of well over 1200mm (47in). Under dif-

ferent names the Chobe and Okavango rivers meander in a parallel course southwards through Angola to cross Namibia's Caprivi Strip. At Mohembo just north of Shakawe the Okavango enters Botswana having changed its name from the Cuito River. For a further 90km (54 miles) the wide, fast-flowing Okavango is hemmed in a narrow flood plain between two parallel fault lines until it pours out onto the flat Kalahari sands, fanning out across the expanse of the Okavango Delta.

The **Thamalakane River** drains the Okavango Delta, carrying the minuscule overflow through Maun. The two main rivers that drain the east of the country are the **Shashe** and the **Motloutse**. The seasonal flow of the Motloutse has now been dammed to provide water for the towns of eastern Botswana through a massive pipeline stretching across 360km (216 miles) of dry countryside.

Much of the country is flat, savanna grassland with a scattering of thorn and scrub bush, although the south-eastern hardveld has a somewhat varied geology with more reliable rainfall, greater fertility and agricultural potential. As a result, 80% of the country's population lives in this region.

This more densely populated swathe of land constitutes just 20% of the country and runs from Ramokgwebana at the border with Zimbabwe in the

## RIVER OF MANY NAMES

The Chobe River crosses the Caprivi Strip just under 200km (120 miles) east of the Okavango River, but does not actually enter the country; instead this wide watercourse defines the international border between Botswana and Namibia. The Chobe starts its life in Angola as the Kwando River, then becomes the Linyanti as it passes through the Caprivi and feeds the Linyanti Swamps. For a short stretch just before Lake Liambezi it is known as the Itenge, before finally becoming the Chobe.

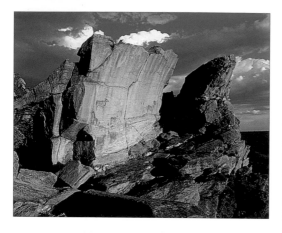

▲ *Above: The famous 'Van der Post's Panel' of ancient San paintings in the Tsodilo Hills.*

east to Ramatlabama on the South African border near Mafikeng in the south. Along its length, hilly ranges and rocky outcrops adorn the landscape.

There are no mountains in Botswana and, apart from the hilly southeast, the only hills of significance are found in the northwest where there are three outcrops. Located in a flat sea of sand, these ranges are of great geological and historical significance.

The most important of these is the **Tsodilo Hills** whose rocky cliffs rise up about 400m (1312ft) above the surrounding plain, and can be seen from the Okavango Delta over 50km (31 miles) away. The Tsodilo Hills are one of the most significant historical rock art sites in the world with as many as 3500 individual paintings charting over 25,000 years of almost continual human habitation in the area.

The **Aha** and **Gcwihaba** hills are approximately 150km (90 miles) southwest of Tsodilo and are extremely remote, involving a challenging 6–7-hour journey by four-wheel-drive vehicle to reach them. Although *Aha* means 'little rocks', these hills form the largest range in northern Botswana, overlooking the dune fields of the Namibian border.

The **Gcwihaba Hills** to the east are part of the same range and are named after an ancient river which used to flow through them. *Gcwihaba* is the !Kung word for 'hyena's lair', and it was this river that created the magnificent **Drotsky's Caves** with their dramatic stalagmites, stalactites and flowstone formations which are also to be found in the range. !Kung is an almost forgotten San dialect spoken in northwestern Botswana.

## TREASURE-TROVE TUNNELS

Overlooking the dunes on Botswana's far western border are the Gcwihaba Hills, in which hide the mysterious Drotsky's Caves. Shown to Martinus Drotsky by the San in 1934, these dramatic caverns are the result of climate changes which, over the eons, have carved out the passages and formed the fantastic flowstones, stalagmites and stalactites. Legend has it that the founder of Ghanzi, Hendrik van Zyl hid his huge fortune of gold and ivory in these caves before he was tried for murder. After his death the treasure was never found and, as yet, these caves remain fully unexplored.

### Inland Waters

As an arid semidesert country with very little usable surface water, it is remarkable that in years of good rain Botswana can suddenly be blessed with immense shallow sheets of water as the huge northern salt pans fill up.

The inflow of the Okavango River alone would be enough to support the needs of a fully industrialized nation, were it not for evaporation. Unfortunately the pressure to harness this water is great – Angola needs the water to set up agricultural projects and Namibia wants to dam the watercourse. However, if the unique river flow is reduced or disturbed in any way, much of the Delta could be threatened. Consequently there is continual lobbying by conservation groups for greater protection of the Delta.

While completely dry for much of the year the major Makgadikgadi pans of **Sua**, **Ntwetwe** and **Nxai**, with their countless smaller companions, do fill with both local rainfall and the inflow of certain rivers such as the Nata and Boteti. As the pans are clay-bottomed, the water is not readily absorbed into the ground and often remains on the surface long into the winter, when the pans become focal points for thirsty birds and wildlife.

These pans are actually the last remains of the great inland lake that covered much of northern Botswana 40,000 years ago. It was fed by the combined inflow of

▼ Below: Palm trees on Chief's Island in the Okavango stand silhouetted against the rising sun.

### FISHING

The north of Botswana is a fisherman's paradise. The resorts at Shakawe in the Okavango Panhandle are famous for **tigerfish** and **bream**, and the length of the Chobe River offers excellent sport fishing. An annual event not to be missed in the northern Okavango near the Panhandle is the '**Barbel Run**'. This occurs between September and October when masses of small fish are forced to swim upstream as the flood plains dry up. The **catfish** (or barbel as they are known locally) attack them in a feeding frenzy, which in turn attracts crocodiles who feed on the catfish. An unforgettable spectacle for both fishermen and photographers.

the Okavango, Chobe and Zambezi rivers, spanning an area of up to 60,000km² (23,160 sq miles) to a maximum depth of 100m (328ft). This area is at the tail end of the Great East African Rift Valley and, being tectonically unstable, the faulting and warping of the earth's crust over the centuries diverted both the Chobe and Zambezi rivers causing the superlake to dry up.

As recently as 1500 years ago there was still water in the lowest levels of the lake, but today all that remains is a flat, sun-baked parchland called the **Makgadikgadi**. Covering 12,000 km² (4632 sq miles) the pans which make up the Makgadikgadi are absolutely featureless, without a single rock or blade of grass. It is this very desolation that has made them into such a tourist attraction, but the pans are also of economic importance: vast deposits of brine are being extracted from Sua Pan for the production of not only salt, but also soda ash for use by the world's glass and chemical manufacturers.

### The Animal Kingdom

Botswana's prime attraction is its abundant bird and wildlife. Over 160 different mammal species have been identified, including the 'big five' – **lion**, **leopard**, **elephant**, **buffalo** and **rhino** – as well as a myriad antelope including the rare aquatic **sitatunga** and **red lechwe**.

▼ *Below: Africa's most endangered carnivore, the wild dog, hunts in packs.*

Over 550 **bird** species have been identified, 400 of which can be seen in the Gaborone area. Several of these birds are extremely rare and are unique to certain areas of Botswana. Best 'birding' areas are the Okavango Delta, the Chobe River from Kazungula to Serondela, the Tuli area and Nata, while an incredible array of raptors can be seen in the Mabuasehube area of the Kgalagadi Transfrontier Park. The best time of year for bird-watching is during the hot summer months when males sport their bright breeding plumage and droves of migrants have arrived.

Although generally shy and seldom encountered, **snakes** remain a concern for tourists and campers. Of the 72 species found in Botswana only 15 are dangerous, and just half of these are deadly. On the other hand, you are likely to see some of the 157 different reptiles and amphibians, particularly crocodiles, lizards, geckos, monitors and frogs.

A bewildering array of flying and crawling insects are to be found in Botswana, but few of them are dangerous or unpleasant. Contrary to popular belief, the most dangerous creatures you are likely to see on your trip are not lions or buffalo, but **mosquitoes**. Antimalaria precautions must be taken.

With their painful bite, **tsetse fly** can be very trying, particularly in the summer months, but one should not forget that it has been their presence that has saved the Okavango from the cattle onslaught. **Scorpions** can also add an unpleasant sting to your trip, so it's a good idea to shake out your shoes before putting them on. They are not deadly and ordinary antihistamine cream provides effective relief, so be sure to pack a tube!

While there are some really impressive **spiders** in Botswana – the fearsome button spider, the eight-eyed jumping spider and the incredible 'golden orb' spider which spins an iridescent golden thread – the only spider that might bite (an unlikely occurrence), and which is responsible for 90% of spider bites in southern Africa, is the innocent-looking little 'sac spider' which spins a noticeable smudgy white nest on curtains and in cupboards. Its painless bite is cytotoxic.

▲ Above: The large granulated rock scorpion (Ischnuridea hadogenes).

### SNAKES ALIVE

Some of the more unfriendly snakes in Botswana include:
● **Egyptian cobra** – mainly in north and east of Botswana; up to 2m (6½ft) in length.
● **Mozambique spitting cobra** – up to 1.5m (5ft) long; nocturnal; found mainly in the Okavango and eastern regions of Botswana.
● **Black mamba** – fearsome, fast and aggressive; up to 2.5m (8ft) long.
● **Puff adder** – widespread; responsible for over 60% of serious bites due to its habit of sunning itself in pathways, where it is stepped on.
● **Boomslang** – a tree snake; maximum length of 2m (6½ft). It occurs throughout most of Botswana.

### THE SAN

The San are the original inhabitants of southern Africa and derive their name from the Bakgothu word meaning 'those who gather wild food'. While their hunter-gatherer way of life has been overrun by modern man, an accurate record of their history has been preserved through the remarkable rock paintings they have left behind. The San believe in a special conservationist relationship between mankind and the nature which sustains them. Their unusual language is characterized by unique 'click' consonants. These are explained in greater detail on page 119.

### HISTORY IN BRIEF

Remains of Palaeolithic man have been discovered throughout southern Africa, pointing to habitation for at least the last million years, but the earliest modern inhabitants of Botswana were the **San** (Bushmen). They have lived an almost unchanged lifestyle in the country since the Middle Stone Age. Having avoided the onslaught of modern man by retreating deeper and deeper into the wastelands, these remarkable people have managed to maintain their individualistic hunter-gatherer existence until as recently as the early 1980s when the last wandering family groups were unwillingly brought into the 'civilized' world.

The San were a peace-loving people who lived in harmony with nature, but not so the more dominant, socially organized **Bantu tribes** that migrated into the subcontinent from the Congo Basin about 1500 years ago. The peaceful San were no match for these tribal groups – who came with their knowledge of pottery, cattle rearing and iron working – and they were quickly conquered, being assimilated as slaves or driven away completely.

The first socially stratified Bantu 'chiefdoms' with a distinct class structure emerged in Botswana a thousand years ago near Palapye and, by AD1200, a second greater power had developed, with its capital on **Mapungubwe Hill** at the confluence of the Shashe and Limpopo rivers in the present-day Mashatu Game Reserve area. This hilltop community was soon eclipsed by the **Great Zimbabwe Empire** which spread its domain over much of eastern Botswana.

Following centuries of tribal nomadism and the endless splitting and

▼ *Below: The scattered thatched huts of a traditional village punctuate the flat Kalahari sandscape.*

reforming of groups of people, almost all the fertile land in southern Africa had been occupied by the early 19th century. As a result the people became competitive, vying for the natural wealth that the land had to offer. Social unrest, tribal tension and chaos, all heightened by the growing ivory and slave trades, ushered in a particularly violent and destructive period in Botswana's history.

▲ *Above: A traditional Zulu village in the time of Shaka and his Impis.*

### The Difaqane Wars

The Difaqane was a devastating wave of tribal wars that swept across much of southern Africa including Botswana in the early 1800s. It started in 1816 in South Africa's KwaZulu-Natal province where a Zulu prince named **Shaka** seized the throne and initiated a series of expansionist wars to extend his powerbase.

This violent upheaval had a domino effect as Shaka's opponents, who fled north, in turn conquered other tribes, sparking off more wars. Untold lives were lost, lands were devastated and the survivors scattered, spreading out across the northern regions of the sub-continent. One of the most notable northern migrations as a result of this turmoil was **Mzilikazi's** odyssey across Botswana to Bulawayo in Zimbabwe where his tribe eventually settled, establishing themselves as the proud Ndebele who still live in that area today.

By 1836 when the Zulu empire was at its peak, 20,000 **Boer Voortrekkers** left the Cape heading north to escape British rule. They too displaced many people, adding to the already confused flood of humanity. Although this tragic Difaqane period lasted just 20 years, countless people died and as many as 100,000 refugees were driven into the arid northwest.

### MZILIKAZI'S ROUTE

In 1822 Mzilikazi, the Zulu king of the Amakhumalo clan, disagreed with Shaka over the ownership of some cattle. As a result he had to flee northwards with 300 of his people. But he was a strong leader and gathered many followers along the way. He eventually settled in the Magaliesburg Mountains where he began building the Amandebele Nation, and by 1830 he controlled all the land between the Vaal and Ngotwane rivers. In 1836 clashes with the Voortrekkers forced him to flee into Botswana, driving the Batswana away before him. In 1840, after four years moving through the country, Mzilikazi and his tribe settled in Bulawayo, leaving the Batswana to return and rebuild their communities.

## Missionaries and Merchants

The London Missionary Society (LMS) was formed in 1795 and by 1808 their first representative, Mr W Edwards, had reached Kanye, but it was not until Moffat set up a permanent mission station at Kuruman in 1821 that Christianity began to spread into Botswana. Much of this was carried by the explorers and traders who wanted to open up the lucrative ivory routes. In 1841 David Livingstone arrived at Kuruman and, within a year, had visited the Bakwena. In 1845 after marrying Moffat's daughter Mary he settled among the Bakwena at Kolobeng where he established the first mission and school in the country; it was from this base that he organized his many trips into the African interior.

**Ivory** was to become Botswana's most sought after commodity and, although an elephant tusk would fetch just over one shilling, there was enough to bring great wealth to the tribes of central Botswana who bought guns to consolidate their power and unite their kingdoms. But even with this firepower they could not stem the growing tide of European traders and settlers who were spearheading the scramble for Africa.

In 1866, **gold** was discovered near Francistown and Africa's first gold rush ensued followed by another a few years later in Zimbabwe, where numerous other richer goldfields were discovered.

## The Threat of Incorporation

The combined problems of colonial pressure and the Boer threat greatly worried the Tswana kings. **Cecil John Rhodes** was also concerned about the Boers and, in an effort to thwart their encroachment, in March 1885 he persuaded the British government to declare Botswana the 'British Protectorate of Bechuanaland'. This saved the country from the Boers, but strengthened Rhodes and his expansionist aspirations to incorporate Bechuanaland into Rhodesia (now Zimbabwe). The people of Botswana were left with the same problem, just a different adversary.

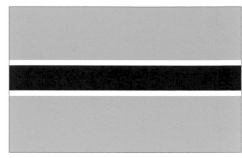

In order to solve this growing dilemma, in 1895, in a daring political move, three Tswana kings, **Khama**, **Bathoen** and **Sebele**, went to England to appeal to the British government not to transfer the Protectorate to Rhodes and his British South Africa Company. While the kings did receive the support of certain antislavery and humanitarian groups, it was only the failed **Jameson Raid** in the last days of 1895 that won them the support of the British government and secured the country's future as a Protectorate, with nominal involvement and interference.

There was a further threat to Bechuanaland's sovereignty in 1910 when the Union of South Africa attempted to incorporate the country, but the vigilant Tswana kings again successfully lobbied for exclusion. The protectorate status was to remain until full independence in 1966 and brought with it a long period of 'peaceful neglect', characterized by little development, but also with few of the colonial impositions suffered by every other country in southern and central Africa.

### The Controversial Khama Marriage

It is sad to think that the best-known episode in Botswana's history was the international campaign to ruin the marriage of Seretse and Ruth Khama.

**Seretse Khama**, the Prince Regent of the Bangwato, met **Ruth Williams** soon after World War II while he was studying law in London. They fell in love and Seretse announced his intention to marry the Englishwoman. Khama's uncle Tshekedi opposed this as it was the Ngwato tradition that a chief's wife should be a Motswana woman chosen by the tribal leaders.

▲ *Above: Botswana's national flag, a symbol of unity and peace in southern Africa.*
◄ *Opposite: Dr David Livingstone, the famous missionary and explorer who brought Christianity to Botswana and much of central Africa.*

## THE NATIONAL FLAG

Unlike many other African flags with stripes of black and red reflecting the wars of liberation, Botswana's national flag is dominated by a tranquil blue. This is an intentional reflection of the peaceful, calm nature of the people, with the black and white stripes a symbol of racial harmony. The blue represents water and rain,.which create prosperity. The black represents the black Batswana and the white represents the white Batswana, so together the flag conveys the ideal of a prosperous multiracial society living together in harmony.

▲ *Above: The village* kgotla *or meeting place.*

▶ *Opposite: Seretse Khama, Botswana's first president.*

## VILLAGE DEMOCRACY

There has always been a democratic tradition among the Batswana in the form of the **kgotla**, or tribal court. This is a place where the common people and their leaders meet to discuss matters of importance and pass judgements. Here all people, regardless of social standing, have a chance to resolve problems. The *kgotla* is usually in the middle of the village under a tree outside the chief's residence. In modern Botswana the village *kgotla* is still the focal point of the community. If you are passing through tribal land and wish to ask permission to camp, or even if you are just seeking the services of a guide, start at the *kgotla* and respectfully ask if you can speak to the **kgosi** (chief). His endorsement will ensure the help of everyone.

The British were also strongly against the marriage, which took place on 29 September 1948. Apart from their own prejudices, they feared that it would offend the administrations in Rhodesia and particularly South Africa with whom the British were anxious to negotiate a plutonium deal. To separate the couple, Seretse was enticed to England on an official invitation and then refused re-entry into his own country.

Soon afterwards Ruth joined Seretse in London where they lived together in exile for five years before being permitted back home in 1956, after Seretse and his children had renounced their claim to chieftainship. But this renunciation left Seretse free to pursue a successful political career.

Soon after his triumphant return he became actively involved in the formation of the Botswana Democratic Party (BDP) and the drive towards independence, as a result of which he was destined to become the first president of Botswana and eventually to be knighted by the Queen of England.

### Independence

Indicative of the lack of interest shown in the Bechuanaland Protectorate by the British, the colony was administered from **Mafikeng** in South Africa, making it one of the few countries in the world to have had its capital outside its national boundaries.

**Sir Charles Rey**, the Commissioner of the Protectorate in the early 1930s, worked vigorously for greater development of the country and was the first advocate for moving the country's capital to within its borders. But this was not to happen until independence some 30 years later.

## HISTORICAL CALENDAR

**25,000BC–AD1000** San occupy Botswana leaving artefacts and rock paintings.
**1000** Bantu peoples move in, displacing the San.
**1100** First hilltop chiefdoms.
**1200** Mapungubwe Hill becomes the most important political centre in the country.
**1400** The Bakgalagadi settle in western Transvaal and eastern Botswana.
**1500** Batswana migrate westward into Botswana.
**1816** Shaka seizes Zulu throne.
**1820** Difaqane Wars begin.
**1830** Mzilikazi betrays Shaka and flees northwest, attacking the Batswana.
**1837** The Voortrekkers drive Mzilikazi into Botswana.
**1841** David Livingstone is the first Christian missionary to enter Botswana.
**1848** Sechele the Paramount

Chief of the Bakwena is converted to Christianity.
**1866** Gold discovered at Tati.
**1872** Khama III installed as Chief of the Ngwato.
**1885** British extend Protectorate status to Bechuanaland.
**1895** Khama, Bathoen and Sebele visit England to stop the transfer of the Protectorate to Rhodes.
**1896** The Jameson Raid fails.
**1921** Seretse Khama born.
**1948** Seretse Khama marries Ruth Williams.
**1950** The multiracial 'Joint Advisory Council' established.
**1956** The Khama family returns from exile.
**1962** The Botswana Democratic Party is formed with Seretse Khama as its leader.
**1963** Construction of the capital city Gaborone begins.
**1966** Botswana gains full

independence, Sir Seretse Khama installed as the first president.
**1967** Diamonds found at Orapa.
**1980** Sir Seretse Khama dies.
**1991** President Dr Ketumile Masire is knighted by Queen Elizabeth II.
**1998** Botswana established as first International Financial Services Centre on mainland Africa. Masire steps down and Festus Mogae becomes Botswana's third President.
**2000** Sedudu Island is confirmed as part of Botswana by the International Court in the Hague.
**2008** Ian Khama, Sir Seretse Khama's eldest son, becomes Botswana's fourth President.
**2011** Botswana welcomes more than 2 million tourists.

In the early 1960s Gaborone was selected as the site of the new capital and frenetic construction began immediately. In 1965 the Bechuanaland Protectorate was granted internal self-government as a prequel to the birth of the Republic of Botswana and full independence on 30 September 1966, under the leadership of Seretse Khama.

Sir Seretse Khama died in 1980 and was succeeded by **Sir Ketumile Masire**. In 1998 Festus Mogae then assumed the presidency for ten years before handing over the reins of power to Ian Khama, Seretse's eldest son, in April 2008.

Having achieved excellent economic growth and political stability since independence, Botswana was able to avoid the effects of the unrest in Rhodesia (now Zimbabwe), South

The central element in Botswana's coat of arms is a shield containing three interlocking **cogs**, which represent industrial progress in all sectors; three **waves** which represent water implying prosperity and peace; and the **head of a cow**, being the traditional symbol of wealth. The shield is supported by two **zebras**, the national animal. One zebra holds a stalk of corn and the other an elephant tusk, symbolizing the important balance between the country's natural resources and agricultural activities. Beneath the coat of arms is a scroll with the word **Pula**. Pula is the Setswana word for rain, which brings prosperity, goodwill and peace.

West Africa (now Namibia) and South Africa, and, with her accumulated wealth, was better able to weather the 2008/09 global recession.

## GOVERNMENT AND ECONOMY

Since independence the **Botswana Democratic Party** (BDP) has governed the country. The British system of parliamentary rule and democracy was inherited by the Botswana government and, under the inspired leadership of Seretse Khama, Botswana was one of the few countries in Africa to choose democracy over socialism at independence.

The head of state is the president who is elected to serve a term of five years by the 61-member National Assembly of Parliament which holds legislative powers and includes the 16 cabinet ministers. The House of Chiefs is made up of 35 chiefs and tribal representatives whose function is to advise the National Assembly on bills affecting tribal organization, customary law and land usage.

Botswana is divided into nine 'districts' each administered separately by a District Commissioner who is responsible for the implementation of the government's various development programmes. Time has proven the failings of socialism and, while many of Botswana's neighbours are restructuring their political and economic systems, Botswana is reaping the benefits of a free-market, capitalist economic policy.

Batswana society is based on a concept of social harmony, which in Setswana is called *kagisano*. This enshrines the ideals of unity, peace, harmony and a sense of community. In the modern political context, *kagisano* still forms an important part of the country's National Development Plan, by determining the four national principles of *Ditiro tsa ditlha-*

▼ *Below: The massive trucks that work in Jwaneng diamond mine's open-cast pit are some of the largest in the world.*

*bololo* (Development), *Boipelego* (Self-reliance), *Popagao ya sechaba* (Unity) and *Puso ya batho ka batho* (Democracy), which are all derived from Batswana culture.

Rather like capitalism, the concept of democracy being enshrined as a national pillar is quite unique in Africa. There has always been an established and active opposition in Botswana's political arena, and the regular elections are contested by a diverse range of parties.

While there are regular cries of foul play and accusations of corruption, the political environment in Botswana is remarkably stable with an adherence to non-violent political negotiation, and *kgotla*-style dialogue.

### A Diamond-studded Economy

Since independence in 1966 Botswana has had the fastest growth in per capita income in the world, with economic growth averaging over 3% per year since 1990 – which it is currently exceeding.

The reason for this phenomenal growth was the discovery of diamonds in 1967. **De Beers** had been prospecting in the country for 12 years prior to this discovery, but even they were not prepared for the significance of the massive diamond reserves in Botswana. Botswana is the world's largest producer of gem quality diamonds, and even with the negative impact of the global recession of 2009, by 2011, from its four large diamond mines – Orapa, Jwaneng, Letlhekane and Damtshaa – the country produced 22.89 million carats of diamonds. This makes Botswana by far the world's leading producer of diamonds by both value and volume.

**Orapa Diamond Mine** went into full production in 1971 following the construction of the mine, the town and a new road network. By 1977, when **Letlhekane Mine** started production, Orapa had become one of the largest diamond mines in the world, but then **Jwaneng** was discovered. Opened in 1982, it is now

▲ *Above: Sorting diamonds, the mainstay of Botswana's burgeoning economy.*

### A BEACON OF HOPE

In 1972, the President, Sir Seretse Khama, said 'Botswana is widely regarded as a beacon of hope in a troubled region, and a force for constructive change. We as a nation, should be an example in the defence and development of non-racialism and social justice for all.' Sir Seretse Khama worked relentlessly at setting this example for other nations to follow and Botswana has indeed remained a shining example of a harmonious non-racial society in a troubled continent.

one of the richest diamond mines in the world.

Diamonds have accounted for a full 75% of Botswana's export earnings; consequently the government has focused on economic diversification initiatives. These included a manufacturing and vehicle assembly drive in the 1990s and is now focusing on the diamond processing industry with the massive 'Diamond City' cutting and polishing complex having been built near Gaborone airport.

In terms of other mining activity there is a big copper nickel mine near Selebi-Phikwe and vast coal deposits in the Serule area which by 2014 are expected to fuel a huge power station at Mmamabua that will help address southern Africa's critical power shortages. The enormous soda ash project on Sua Pan continues to operate in the face of difficult world prices and periodic flooding, while in 2003 the discovery of new gold deposits east of Francistown brought new life to the country's gold-mining industry.

## Wildlife and Tourism

Tourism is a significant foreign exchange earner, currently generating 9% of total GDP and 10% of national employment, much of it in the rural areas. In the past hunting was the main contributor to the industry, but now there is a strong emphasis on photographic and ecotourism.

Although tourism already provides 40% of formal employment in the north of the country, it is still a major growth industry, and with the government's continual development of land usage plans and new area allocations, opportunities are always becoming available for tourism entrepreneurs. Scores of operators in Botswana offer anything from self-drive or

## BOTSWANA AND THE RECESSION OF 2009

Botswana banks were reasonably isolated with limited exposure to the 'credit crunch' of 2009. But the resultant collapse in global diamond sales had a very severe effect on the country's economy with the value of total exports being slashed by almost 25% by the middle of 2009. Fortunately by then Botswana had accumulated massive savings and forward cover which was able to sustain the country through its huge budget deficit of 2009/2010 while still being able to maintain an investment grade rating of A/A-1. Botswana is now proudly ranked as having the best credit rating in Africa, and with diamond sales and tourism both picking up, Botswana's economy is once again sparkling.

guided safari vehicle hire to elephant-back safaris, but to preserve the country's pristine environment the government's stated policy of low-volume, high-cost tourism remains. Thus, while Botswana may be more expensive than Kenya or other high-volume safari destinations, it is still a politically stable, exclusive and unspoiled destination which, through careful management, is likely to remain so.

The Department of Wildlife and National Parks (DWNP), which administers all of the national parks and conservation areas in Botswana, sets various conditions for visitors to abide by for both their own safety and the well-being of the wildlife. But as conditions change and tourist pressure increases, these regulations are updated regularly. For example, no driving is allowed in Botswana's national parks outside of the prescribed opening hours, camping is only permitted in designated camp sites, and all overnight visits to national parks must be pre-booked and pre-paid. The DWNP has also recently privatized many camp sites, so you may need to check who the relevant booking agent is by contacting the DWNP offices in Gaborone (tel: +267 318 0774) or Maun (tel: +267 686 1265), or via e-mail: parks.reservations.gaborone@gov.bw

### CITES BAN

With the international ban on the trade of elephant products, African elephant populations have recovered, moving from 'endangered' to 'vulnerable'. But Botswana still has far too many elephants for its fragile ecosystem, especially in Chobe and Moremi, and has been pushing CITES for a limited legalization of the ivory trade. Unfortunately until a decision is made Botswana has to continue managing its elephant population with culls.

◄ *Opposite: Elephant-back safaris offer an exciting and unique way of seeing the Okavango Delta.*
▼ *Below: A commercial cattle rancher inspecting his free-range herd.*

### Ranching and Agriculture

With persistent drought and soaring summer temperatures, only 0.61% of Botswana is considered to be arable land with 0.02% of the country used for permanent crops of which less than 25km² (11 square miles) is under irrigation. Yet almost the entire rural population is involved in either subsistence farming of maize and sorghum or livestock rearing.

▲ *Above: Mechanized commercial agriculture is limited to the southeastern corridor of Botswana.*

There are a few commercial farms in the Tuli Block as well as tracts of cultivated land around Gaborone, Pandamatenga and Kasane where a variety of crops and fruit is grown. Production is limited, however, and while certain food products such as pasta are exported to South Africa, the country still imports the majority of its food.

Cattle ranching is much more successful, with vast areas producing excellent free-range beef, with the Ghanzi area reputedly being the finest ranchland in the world. As a revenue earner the industry was originally second only to mining, but with the diversification of the economy in the 1990s, manufacturing and financial services have surpassed the beef industry. However, cattle are still a symbol of wealth in traditional Batswana society where a man's social standing is reflected in the size of his herd. Cattle still outnumber people in Botswana by at least 2 to 1. This volume of cattle is, however, resulting in widespread overgrazing of the fragile grasslands.

The **Botswana Meat Commission** handles all beef exports from Botswana, the quality of which is world renowned, although the industry has struggled over the last five years, firstly due to the global recession, drought and then with outbreaks of foot-and-mouth disease which ended the country's preferential trade agreement to supply beef to Europe. In Lobatse, where the beef industry is based, there is also a canning factory and a tannery which supplies top quality leather to, amongst others, the Italian shoe and fashion industries.

## Manufacturing

To reduce its dependence on the diamond market and to increase employment of Batswana, the government has tried to encourage investment in the manufacturing industry. These measures have included tax holidays, financial assistance and even across-the-board tax reductions. They have achieved some success, with **rapid growth** of the sector which has seen an incredible 8% annual growth over the last few years. Botswana's manufacturing sector now employs more people than mining does.

Locally manufactured goods include polished diamonds, metal products, plastics, electrical products, chemicals, vaccines, soap, shoes, building materials, food and drink. In addition there are several vehicle assembly plants which supply trucks and buses to the local market.

## THE PEOPLE

Just over two million people from numerous tribes and backgrounds live in Botswana, but despite this diversity, remarkable unity has been achieved as almost everyone considers themselves to be Batswana first, and tribespeople second.

The largest tribal group in Botswana is the original **Tswana** tribe, which still comprises almost 50% of the entire population, followed by the **Bakalanga** people who occupy the northeast and central districts of Botswana where they have lived for almost 1000 years.

The riverine tribes of the **Bayei**, **Basubiya** and **Hambukushu** inhabit the Okavango and Chobe waterways in Ngamiland District, subsisting on the water

### DISEASE CONTROL

In 1896 rinderpest killed hundreds of thousands of animals in Botswana including both cattle and wildlife. This lead to the establishment of the Veterinary Department in 1905, but it was only after the outbreak of foot-and-mouth disease in the late 1970s that the Botswana Vaccine Institute was established to control and eradicate the disease. With the development of the beef industry and access to the European markets through the Lomé agreement, Botswana set up thousands of kilometres of cordon fences to separate cattle from the disease-carrying buffalo. These strict, often unpopular measures have protected the national herd from foot-and-mouth disease (FMD), but tragically since then there have been outbreaks of lung disease, and recently FMD resulting in thousands more cattle having to be destroyed.

▼ *Below: Herero women in their beautiful, but impractical, traditional dresses.*

*▲ Above: A San family works at traditional crafts.*

and its rich natural resources. The Bayei were the first to arrive in the 1700s, closely followed by the Basubiya who established their capital at Luchindo on the Chobe River. The Hambukushu are master basket weavers who are recent additions to the cultural tapestry of Botswana. They arrived in waves from Namibia and Angola over the past couple of hundred years, with the last group of 4000 moving into the country in 1969 to escape the Angolan civil war.

The **Bakgalagadi** tribe are also of Sotho-Tswana origin and are closely related to the Batswana people, sharing similar customs and beliefs. Many Bakgalagadi still practise subsistence agriculture and often occupy the 'Remote Area Dweller' category.

The **San** are also deep rural dwellers who shy away from contact with the larger villages with which they are unfamiliar. However, now that they are no longer able to pursue their traditional hunter-gatherer lifestyles, they rely on government assistance programmes.

### The Changing Lifestyle of the San

There is a common misconception that the San are on the verge of extinction with just a few isolated family groups wandering the Central Kalahari. On the contrary, Botswana has a growing San population of up to 60,000 but their hunter-gatherer way of life is now extinct and they are reeling from tremendous social and cultural change. These changes have deprived the San of their cultural independence and have destroyed their social structure, leaving many of them in extreme poverty, dependent on an undignified existence of government handouts and vulnerable to

## SOUTHWARD MIGRATION

The Bantu-speaking people of southern Africa are believed to have originated from the central rainforests of Gabon and Cameroon about 2500 years ago when there was a rapid population explosion and the tribes began to migrate. First they moved towards the Great Lakes of central Africa and then turned southwards, arriving in Zimbabwe and the east coast of South Africa in about AD200, bringing with them cattle, small stock and the knowledge of both pottery and iron-working. Within several hundred years these people had come to dominate the subcontinent, which had been well populated with a rich tribal tapestry and a widespread network of chiefdoms.

exploitation and racial prejudice.

In addition to these various tribes, there is a significant group of white Batswana, comprised of descendants of the original missionaries, farmers and traders who have permanently settled in the country over the last 100 years.

### The Tswana

Essentially pastoralists for whom cattle are extremely important, the Tswana people who form the majority of the country's population have given their tribal name, with the plural prefix 'Ba' to describe the people of Botswana – hence the term 'Batswana'. In Botswana there are three main groups: the Bakwena ('Crocodile' people) who live in the Molepolole area, the Bangwaketse who live in the Kanye area, and the Bangwato who live in the Palapye and Serowe areas and to whom the Khama family belongs.

### The Traditional Dress of the Herero

The Herero originated in Namibia and only recently moved into the north of the country around Lake Ngami in 1904–1905 to escape the Germans.

The remarkable traditional dresses that Herero woman wear are the result of a German missionary's zealous wife Mrs Emma Hahn, who – 150 years ago – wanted to eliminate nudity amongst Herero women, so taught them to sew. The Herero women copied the Victorian-style dresses that the missionary wives wore, making their own adaptations, including the bright colours and the two-pointed headdress, which represents a young cow's horns.

Herero women still sew these dresses, using up to 10m (33ft) of fabric to make the pleated skirt, and reams of material to make the numerous petticoats. The outfits are heavy and impractical,

## A Tolerant People

Having been spared the full effects of colonial rule, and with a tradition of providing refuge for any displaced people, Batswana are well known for their relaxed, welcoming attitude and their remarkable racial and tribal tolerance. Over the last 100 years this has made Botswana one of the most peaceful countries on the African continent. As a result Botswana has also been spared the ravages of civil wars and liberation struggles that have marred the history of all her neighbours. Botswana even provided safe haven for Yugoslavian refugees during their civil war of the late 1990s.

▼ Below: A San hunter uses his traditional light bow and poisoned arrows, coupled with his incredible stealth and tracking skills.

## Speak the Language

These phrases might come in handy when conversing with the local peoples:

**Hello sir/madam** •
*Dumela Rra/Mma*
**Hello gentlemen/ladies** •
*Dumelang borra/bomma*
**How are you?** • *Le kae?*
**I am fine** • *Ke teng*
**Stay well** (said when you're leaving) • *Sala sentle*
**Travel well** (said when someone else is leaving) •
*Tsamaya sentle*
**No problem** • *Ga gona mathata*
**Thank you** • *Ke itumetse/tanki*
**Okay/Good-bye** • *Go siame*
**No** • *Nnyaa*
**Yes** • *Ee*
**Petrol** • *Lookwae/Peterolo*
**Bread** • *Borotho/Senkgwe*
**Water** • *Metsi*
**I want to see the doctor** •
*Ke batla go bona ngaka*
**How much does this cost?** • *Ke bo kae?*

especially in summer, but one will often see women in their traditional dress, especially in Maun. However, remember that if you want to take photographs of Herero women in traditional dress, it is important to ask permission first and a small fee is usually charged.

## Language

Setswana is the national language and all the major tribes speak it with minor differences in dialect. This contributes to their tribal harmony. However, English is the official business language and it is widely spoken in the urban areas with most written communication being in this language. In certain rural areas and smaller commercial centres Afrikaans is often used. This is as a result of the significant number of Batswana who were employed as migrant labour on the mines in South Africa.

## Religion

While **Christianity** is now the official religion in Botswana, and certainly the strongest, with well over 60% of the population abiding by its tenets, a variety of different faiths are also practised. Certain traditional beliefs have been incorporated into modern Christianity, such as the concept of *Modimo*, the supreme being. The Zion Christian Church is the strongest denomination, and its

followers can be identified by the small felt-backed silver star that they wear.

Christianity was brought into Botswana by **David Livingstone** in the middle of the 19th century and **Sechele I**, the Chief of the Bakwena was the first Motswana to be converted to Christianity. This conversion was probably more as a result of shrewd political – rather than spiritual – motivation in an attempt to secure British support and approval, as at his conversion the chief remarked to Livingstone, 'If you like I shall call my headmen and, with our whips, we shall soon make them all believe.'

There is a strong **Muslim** community in Botswana, while in Gaborone North there is a **Buddhist** Meditation Centre where there grows a seedling of the original 'Bo' fig tree (*Ficus religiosa*), under which Prince Siddhartha, the founder of Buddhism, gained 'enlightenment' or *bodhi* some 2500 years ago.

### Food and Drink

Wholesome traditional food is available in most restaurants throughout Botswana and for foreign visitors it is well worth a try, even though some of it, such as dried **mopane worms** (highly nutritious with an appealing nutty flavour) may require an open mind and a strong will. **Seswaa** is the traditional beef dish and is served with *pap*, which is a soft maize meal.

Traditional **beer** is also very popular – and potent – usually being served from a large clay pot into hollow gourds. Unlike western beers it is not clear, but has a distinct texture. *Chibuku* is the commercially brewed version of this beer and, although very low in alcohol, is interesting for its unfamiliar lumpy consistency. In a calculated government policy to protect the income of many otherwise unemployed women, this cardboard-cartonned drink is not available in official liquor stores, and can only be bought from the *shebeens*. Ask your local guide where you can buy some as it is definitely worth a taste.

In Ngamiland around the Okavango and Makgadikgadi areas, where the real fan palm (*Hyphaene petersiana*) and wild date palms (*Phoenix reclinata*) are common, a very intoxicating **palm wine** known locally as *muchema* is distilled from their sap. Unfortunately, this is not easily found as the tapping process often leads to the death of the trees, which are also under threat from the commercial basket weavers who reap the new leaves of these palms to make their wares.

▲ *Above: For the gourmet with a strong constitution, the mopane worm offers an interesting alternative to everyday fare.*
◀ *Opposite: The imposing, buttressed London Missionary Society church in Serowe.*

## CULTURAL AWARENESS

In Botswana you'll notice many interesting customs, such as the way people hand things to each other with one hand grasping the other wrist to show they are not concealing a weapon behind their back. You may also be surprised by the way men push in front of women through doors and lifts. Unlike in Western culture, in traditional Batswana society men always go through doors first to ward off impending danger on the other side. So remember if a man pushes in front of you, it might not be because he's being disrespectful!

# 2
# Gaborone and Surrounds

As one of Africa's fastest growing cities, **Gaborone**, Botswana's capital, is a vibrant, colourful metropolis. Due to its phenomenal growth from an obscure village in the early 1960s to home to almost 500,000 people in just 40 years, Gaborone has neither a long history nor an established traditional African character, as other African cities such as Dar es Salaam and Nairobi do. But Gaborone still provides all the facilities you would expect to find in any modern city.

The tiny administrative village of Gaberone's (literally 'Gaberone's place') was selected in 1964 as the site of the country's new capital primarily because of its reliable water supply, its strategic location and its proximity to the 'Cape to Cairo' railway line.

The city is named after **Chief Gaberone** who lead the Batlokwa tribe into the area in the 1880s. They settled in Tlokweng, the first urban area you reach when driving into the city from the South African border post 20km (12 miles) to the east. In the early 1890s a colonial fort was built by Rhodes's British South Africa Company in the area now known as The Village near Tlokweng. It was from here that the unsuccessful **Jameson Raid** was launched by Cecil John Rhodes in December 1895, sparking the Boer War. At the time there was little more than a handful of buildings in the area.

When Botswana gained independence from Britain on 30 September 1966, Gaborone had just the administrative essentials and a mere 1000 new homes. Two years later it was declared a city and has continued to grow at a rapid pace ever since.

## DON'T MISS

**\*\*\* Mokolodi Game Reserve:** elephant-back encounters, giraffe tracking, cheetah visits and horseback safaris.
**\*\*\* Tracking rhino** through the Mokolodi Hills.
**\*\*\* Gaborone Game Reserve:** for a barbecue breakfast.
**\*\* Matsieng's** footprints and rock engravings
**\*\* Gaborone Dam:** perfect for fishing or picnicking.
**\*\* National Museum and Art Gallery:** Botswana baskets and other exhibitions.
**\*** A climb up **Kgale Hill**.
**\* Shopping:** Game City and River Walk.

◀ *Opposite: A regal Seretse Khama in front of the parliament buildings.*

**31**

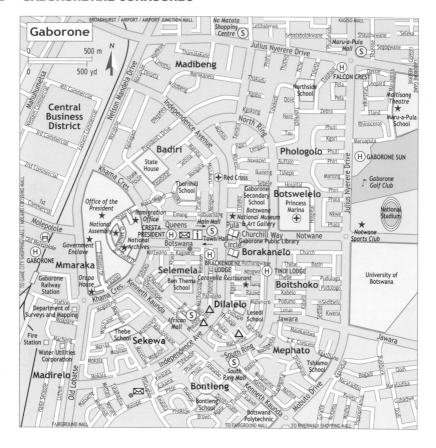

## GABORONE

Gaborone is generally the point of entry into Botswana, through the bustling Sir Seretse Khama International Airport or through its road links with South Africa, providing access for tourists to the main attractions of the Okavango Delta, the Chobe, Tuli Block and the more remote desert areas.

Built around an original circular layout, Gaborone has since experienced frenetic growth. This can be appreciated in the disjointed and confusing layout of the city's roads and suburbs.

The city, which houses the SADC Head Office and the 'Diamond Technology Park', offers a range of modern hotels, casinos, cinemas, a choice of good restaurants and nightclubs. Many of these nightclubs host live performances by the popular artists of Botswana's burgeoning music industry. There are many well-patronized venues offering live music across Gaborone and Mogoditshane 4km (2.5 miles) northeast of the capital.

### A Shopping Paradise **

With its initial focus on establishing the administrative essentials, Gaborone initially didn't have a reputation as a great place to shop. But as a result of growing national prosperity, massive population growth and consumer demand, this has changed and now Gaborone has more retail shopping space per person than almost any other city in the world. For the visitor there is now an amazing choice of modern shopping malls, all laced with trendy restaurants and coffee shops, each vying for the shopper's attention with top quality imported and local products. 'Must visit' malls in Gaborone include the massive **Game City** at the base of Kgale Hill, **Riverwalk Shopping Mall** on the north bank of the Ngotwane River, **BBS Mall** in Broadhurst, the **Main Mall** in the centre of town, the bustling **African** and **Fairground** malls, **Molapo Crossing** and the new **Airport Junction** shopping centre.

### The National Assembly **

The National Assembly is at the top of the Main Mall where it is surrounded by the other tall government buildings. At the centre of this government enclave is a paved square with a War Memorial for those Batswana who gave their lives for the British Empire, and a statue of Sir Seretse Khama, Botswana's first president.

▲ *Above: Vendors and crafts-men display their wares under the shady trees of Gaborone's paved central Mall.*

### BIRD LIFE BOTSWANA

For a fascinating insight into the rich bird life that Botswana has to offer, the Gaborone-based 'Bird Life Botswana' club is very active with regular bird walks on the first Sunday of every month. To join them, meet at Molapo Crossing at 06:30 (or 08:00 in winter). The club also organizes frequent presentations by well-known ornithologists. Excursions are usually advertised in the weekly *Advertiser*, and visitors are welcome. The club can be contacted on tel: 319 0540, or visit www. birdlifebotswana.org.bw

*▲ Above: In the grounds of the National Museum, off Gaborone's busy Independence Avenue, a traditional Batswana hut provides a 'live exhibit' for visitors.*

On the eastern side of the Mall next to the Town Hall is the **Gaborone Public Library**. It boasts a wide selection of books covering all aspects of Botswana's history, people and culture – as does the **British Council**. The Library is open Monday to Friday from 09:00 to 16:30 and Saturdays from 09:00 to 12:00.

### National Sports Centre *

The impressive National Sports Centre is just 2km (1.5 miles) east of the Main Mall on Nyerere Drive between the Gaborone Golf Club and the University of Botswana. League football matches are played here most weekends and it was an official training venue for the 2010 FIFA World Cup. Next to the stadium are the Botswana Tennis Association courts, which have hosted the international Davis Cup competition; the Cricket Club grounds (which host the annual Guy Fawkes fireworks display); and the Squash Club courts. All the courts are open to the public daily, although can generally only be booked by club members.

### National Museum and Art Gallery ***

The National Museum and Art Gallery displays a collection of traditional crafts and paintings by local and regional artists. Their botanical garden is the burial place of the controversial 'El Negro', a mounted Bushman (San) displayed in the Darder Museum of Banyoles in Spain from 1926–97. His remains were returned to Botswana in 2000. Open Tuesday to Friday 09:00 to 18:00 and Saturday and Sunday 09:00 to 17:00; tel: 367 4616.

The **Thapong Visual Arts Centre** in The Village (tel: 316 1771) has a range of arts and crafts, while **Gallery Ann** (tel: 7138 0404) in the Craft Workshop off Nakedi Rd in Broadhurst specializes in paintings.

---

### CRAFT MARKETS

*** **Lentswe-la-Oodi Weavers** in Oodi village about 20km (12 miles) from Gaborone on the Francistown road. Tour the factory and buy colourful ethnic wall hangings and tapestries.

** **Botswana Craft**, on the Western Bypass towards the airport traffic circle, specializes in southern African curios and Botswana baskets.

* **Craft Workshop Flea Market**, on the last Sunday morning of each month, sells up-market ornaments.

* **Informal street market** under the shady trees of the Main Mall.

**Theatres ★★**

There are several established performing arts venues, the main one being the **Maitisong Cultural Centre**. Maitisong is at Maru-a-Pula school, and hosts the **National Maitisong Festival** in March/April plus numerous performances organized throughout the year. There is also a very active local drama group called **Capital Players**. Details of these and other performances by traditional dance and drama groups can be found in the weekly *Advertiser*.

**Gaborone Game Reserve ★★★**

This 550ha (1359-acre) reserve was opened in 1988 through the efforts of the Kalahari Conservation Society, and is now Botswana's third-busiest reserve. It provides an ideal getaway for those wanting to escape the stresses of urban life.

There is a small entrance fee and visitors can see a remarkable range of wildlife including zebra, eland, kudu, red hartebeest, impala and warthog. A detailed route map is supplied at the entrance gate, a short distance off Limpopo Drive on the western side of the city.

Bird-watching in the Gaborone Game Reserve is excellent, particularly in ponds and marshlands along the eastern edge of the park. There are two well-maintained picnic sites and a game hide. Open daily 06:30–18:30.

**Mokolodi Game Reserve ★★★**

This 5000ha (12,355-acre) reserve was established in 1994 by the Mokolodi Wildlife Foundation as both a game reserve and an Environmental Eduction Centre where school-children can be taught the importance of conservation.

Set in a wide valley between the **Mokolodi Hills** and 'Magic Mountain' – inhabited by leopard and porcupine – this scenic reserve has a well-developed network of game-viewing drives. The roads that link the dams and hilltops can be a bit rough in places so 4x4 vehicles are recom-

---

### THE NO. 1 LADIES' DETECTIVE AGENCY

*The No. 1 Ladies' Detective Agency* is one of a charming series of books by Alexander McCall Smith. Set in Gaborone, the book follows the adventures of Mma Ramotswe as she tackles social and cultural issues as well as a touch of real crime. This book, which Laura Bush claims to be her favourite, has been made into a very popular BBC TV series which was directed by Sidney Pollack and which has won wide international acclaim. Many of the film's locations have become tourist landmarks and there are even tour companies offering 'Mma Ramotswe' tours to places like Zebra Drive and the 'Kgale shopping centre'. To arrange tours to the film set itself, tel: 72 654 323.

▼ *Below: A full-grown white rhinoceros (*Ceratotherium simum*), although less aggressive than the black rhino, still weighs in at over 2000kg (4400 lb).*

## EXCELLENT GUIDED WALKS

The Mokolodi Game Reserve is famous for its **guided walks**. Take advantage of the rare opportunity to track rhino or to walk through the bush with young elephants. Excursions are with professional guides and offer outstanding photographic opportunities. A hide at the edge of the elephants' bathing pool allows one to get within feet of these creatures. The walks also give visitors a chance to spot the mountain reedbuck, unique to Mokolodi. Booking is essential.

mended. There is a remarkable abundance of wildlife in the wooded park and visitors can expect to see elephant, rhino, giraffe, zebra, wildebeest, hartebeest, spotted hyena, plentiful impala as well as hand-reared cheetah.

Just 14km (9 miles) west of Gaborone, Mokolodi offers numerous guided walks and **game drives**, including memorable rhino and giraffe tracking through the thick bush. Bicycle trails and horse safaris with trained field guides are also available as are day and night game drives. These evening drives, which can incorporate a fantastic 'bush braai' dinner, are good for spotting the more unusual nocturnal creatures.

There are five **self-catering chalets** set on the edge of a little grass-edged water hole, much favoured by the endangered rhino. At the Alexander McCall Smith Rest Camp guests can stay in traditional Tswana huts or can choose from a range of camp sites. Mokolodi also boasts one of Gaborone's finest restaurants, a bar and a curio shop, and provides transfers to and from the park.

**Gaborone and Surrounds**

### Gaborone Dam ★★

Surrounded by high hills and thick game-filled bush, the setting for 'Gabs Dam' is very attractive. On the southern bank is the 'City Scapes' picnic site near the Kalahari Fishing Club, while the Gaborone Yacht Club has a clubhouse and swimming pool set on a rocky island. With spectacular views over the water and the distant mountains, the club is great for sundowners and light meals.

Temporary membership is available for visitors interested in the water sports that include sailing, canoeing and rowing. For details see www.gyc.org.bw

Gaborone Dam is a good fishing venue where bass, bream and barbel (catfish) can be caught. It is also popular with birders for its wide range of water birds and bee-eaters. Be aware that there is a danger of bilharzia and crocodiles, so swimming in the dam should be avoided.

### Kgale Hill **

Gaborone is dominated by Kgale Hill and it offers a pleasant climb with breathtaking views of the dam and city. Visitors can choose one of three well-defined routes up the hill starting from the parking area opposite the satellite station. They are the steep **Rusty's Route**; the longer **Transfeldt Trail**; and the walk across the saddle to **Cross Kopje**. Each takes less than an hour.

There is a resident troop of baboons living on Kgale and a pair of black eagles consistently nests in the craggy cliff face just below the peak. There have also been reports of early morning sightings of leopard. But, before leaving your car at the base of the hill, it is worth hiring someone from Old Naledi to guard your vehicle as there have been instances of petty theft in the car park area.

### ALONG THE FRANCISTOWN ROAD

There are a few traditional villages north of Gaborone on the Francistown road which are famous for their craft centres and are well worth a visit.

### Phakalane *

From the airport traffic circle take the Francistown road for 8km (5 miles) to the Phakalane turn-off which is on the right. The main attraction here is the **Phakalane Golf Estate Hotel Resort**. It offers a beautifully designed international standard 18-hole golf course with a multimillion dollar clubhouse including the famous Drotsky's fine

▲ *Above: The king of all the beasts*, Panthera leo *surveys his domain.*

## THE BOER WAR

After the **Battle of Crocodile Pools** just outside Gaborone in 1899, the British police and officials stationed at Gaborone were ordered to retreat and destroy the administrative camp there. The only article left of value was a huge safe, but when the Boers who had overrun the area blew it open, all they found was a piece of paper with the words 'sold again!' But not all the war history of Gaborone was so amusing. A bitter battle was fought in the Crocodile Pools area on the hills near Mokolodi overlooking the Metswemaswaane River. Heavy artillery was used by both sides, numerous soldiers were killed, a VC was awarded and the railway bridge over the river was blown up. Grave sites can still be found on the hill on the eastern side of the bridge.

dining restaurant, Feather's Halfway House and Oriental Cuisine, and the elegant Linyanti Bar and lounge.

In addition to the 80 rooms of the four-star hotel there are 12 'Eagle's Nest' luxury villas and eight self-catering chalets available. The golf estate also has a driving range, pro shop and an up-market residential estate lining the greens.

### Mochudi **

Another 10km (6 miles) along the road is the village of Mochudi. This is a place of significant cultural history where tourists will find examples of decorated Setswana architecture, real Batswana *seswaa*, the most southerly baobabs in Botswana, and traditional crafts including the **Ithukeng Tin Workshop**.

The **Phuthadikobo Museum** set on the peak of Phuthadikobo Hill is the centrepiece of the Muchudi Cultural Precinct and with its dramatic cliff-top views is well worth a visit. It records the history of the Kgatleng District and the local Bakgatla people with exhibits, artefacts and original photographs. Guided walking tours are offered to nearby fortifications, decorated homes and the tribal Police Station built in 1872, which is one of the oldest buildings in Botswana. A screen-printing workshop and a traditional blacksmith form part of the museum. Open weekdays 08:00–17:00, weekends 14:00–17:00.

### Matsieng's Footprints ***

This remarkable **cultural heritage site** can be found just north of the village of **Rasesa** at the end of the dual carriageway about 50km (30 miles) outside Gaborone. The sacred **rainmaking site** is one of only four known 'creation' sites in Botswana and is situated close to the main road along a flat 450-million-year-old sandstone stretch of ancient river bed.

▶ *Opposite: Matsieng's actual 'Creation Hole', which never dries up.*

▼ *Below: Brightly coloured woven wall hangings from the Lentswe-la-Oodi Weavers who are based in the village of Oodi depict traditional village scenes.*

There is a series of deep sculptured **potholes** in the watercourse, and out of one, according to local legend **Matsieng** (the 'Adam' of Batswana folklore) emerged, followed by his people and all the animals. Their fading footprints, etched thousands of years ago into the smooth rock, can still be seen coming out of the permanent waters of the pothole.

In addition to the San rock engravings the site also has incredible **geology**, including a scattering of unexplained white 'circles' embedded across the dark rock – any theories are welcome! Entrance to the site is free of charge and the enthusiastic and knowledgeable curator makes a visit to the site well worthwhile.

### WEST OF GABORONE

The villages to the west of Gaborone are set in scenic, hilly country and are rich in crafts and history.

### Kolobeng **

The Kanye road crosses the Kolobeng River 40km (25 miles) from Gaborone. Immediately after the bridge, on the left, is a short dirt road to the **Livingstone Memorial** and the ruins of David Livingstone's house and mission, built in the 1840s. The **church,** the first in Botswana, was where Chief Sechele was converted to Christianity. It was also the first school and the site of the first irrigation project. The foundations of these buildings can still be seen, as can the graves of Livingstone's daughter and the artist Thomas Dolman, both buried on the banks of the river.

▲ *Above: The Thamaga Pottery shop has gained local fame for the high quality of its wares.*

### Bahurutshe Cultural Village ★★★

Near the Livingstone Memorial on the A10 highway is the turn-off to Mmankodi village, which is less than 5km (3 miles) to the south. Just beyond the village in the Nyangani Hills is the remarkable Bahurutshe Cultural village and lodge. Accommodation is in *en-suite* thatched huts and camp sites and guests can experience real traditional life and the rituals of dance, story telling, and share Setswana dishes in a genuine village setting.

### Thamaga ★★

About 12km (7 miles) after Kolobeng is the village of Thamaga. Beyond the Botswelelo Centre is the famous **Thamaga Pottery shop** which produces decorated African pottery of the highest standard. This shop is the hub of a burgeoning local pottery industry.

On the other side of Thamaga the road passes through the **Polokwe Viewing Point** and joins the Trans-Kalahari Highway. North is the rich diamond mine of **Jwaneng** while to the south is the town of Kanye and a link through to Lobatse.

### SOUTHWEST OF GABORONE
### Kanye ★

This sprawling, picturesque village is the capital of the Bangwaketsi tribe. It was founded by **Chief Makaba** in the late 18th century as a well-defended hilltop settlement (its name means 'to destroy' or 'to strike down'). The village was often under siege by various attackers, including **Mzilikazi** on his migration to Bulawayo and the German maverick **Jan Bloem**. But Kanye survived them all and is now an important and prosperous urban centre.

There are some good **traditional restaurants** in Kanye serving unique Batswana dishes. The **Ko Gae** ('My Home') café is situated in the Main Kanye Mall and offers very genuine cuisine. A must are their popular **Seswaa** dishes – boiled and pounded beef being a local favourite often served at traditional celebrations such as weddings.

## Lobatse *

Lobatse, now home to some 80,000 people, was once considered to become Botswana's capital. Named after Chief Molebatse, Lobatse is home to the **Botswana Meat Commission**. Established in 1966 the Commission has a large abattoir, meat canning factory and leather tannery in Lobatse, as well as abattoirs in Francistown and Maun, from where they export quality 'Botswana Beef' to South Africa and various other countries throughout the world.

On the main road between Gaborone and Lobatse is the **St Claire Lion Park Resort**. Although the lions are long gone, there is now a very popular '**water world**' with swimming pools, water slides and a 'luna park' specially designed for children. An entrance fee is charged and in addition to the rides and slides refreshments and fast food are available.

## Otse and the Manyelanong Game Reserve **

The village of Otse is 15km (9 miles) outside Lobatse on the Gaborone road. North of the village is Otse Hill, the highest point in Botswana at 1489m (4885ft) above sea level. In the sheer cliffs beyond the settlement, the tiny Manyelanong Game Reserve protects a breeding colony of **Cape vultures**. The winter months are the best time to visit this reserve. There are now just under 50 breeding pairs of birds in the colony, but it is still one of the largest colonies of vultures in Botswana.

To get to the reserve, turn off the main Lobatse/Gaborone road in Otse at the Moeding College signpost. At the 'Y' junction turn right and keep heading for the high rocky hill.

**THE SOURCE OF THE LIMPOPO**

As described by Rudyard Kipling, the Limpopo River is a 'great gray-green greasy' expanse of coursing water surging across three countries towards the Indian Ocean. It is little known that the source of the Limpopo is just south of Gaborone near Lobatse, where it is called the Ngotwane River. As the Ngotwane River it forms the border between Botswana and South Africa, up to the Ngotwane Dam. This spills directly into the Gaborone Dam, from where the river continues its northeastern journey towards Parr's Halt. Here it changes its name to the Limpopo and again forms the national boundary up to the far eastern tip of the country where Botswana, Zimbabwe and South Africa meet at the confluence of the Limpopo and Shashe rivers.

▼ Below: Cape vultures (Gyps coprotheres) rest in a tree far from their cliff-edge roost.

## BEST TIMES TO VISIT

Gaborone can be oppressively **hot** in summer from **October** to **April**, with temperatures often reaching 38°C (100°F). It can get especially hot between the intermittent **rainstorms**, which fall mainly between **December** and **February**. With Gaborone being relatively low lying (1000m/3281ft above sea level), the summer nights are also hot, with an average drop in temperature of just 10°C (18°F). Winter can be cold, especially at night. Winter days are generally cool and cloudless.

## GETTING THERE

Air Botswana flies daily between Francistown, Maun and Kasane. International routes include Johannesburg, Cape Town, Harare, Victoria Falls, Blantyre, Lilongwe and Nairobi. Contact **Air Botswana Central Reservations** on tel: 368 0900, or check their website at www.airbotswana.co.bw **South African Airways** (tel: 390 2210), **South African Express** (tel: 397 2397) and **Kenya Airways** (tel: 390 5094) all offer direct flights to Gaborone. Many of the international airlines fly out of Johannesburg and Nairobi, connecting Botswana with the world. In addition to air travel, Gaborone is just 360km (224 miles) from Johannesburg with good road and rail links.

## GETTING AROUND

There are several **car-hire** companies in Gaborone: **Avis**, tel: 391 3039, e-mail: botswanares@avis.co.bw; **Budget**, tel: 390 2030, fax: 390 2028; **Limit Car Rentals**, tel: 393 2825, e-mail: limitcar@botsnet.bw; **Select Car Rental**, tel: 397 1240, fax: 390 1141. Several **air charter** companies offer scheduled or special charters flights to tourists and business destinations. They include **Kalahari Air Services**, tel: 395 1804, e-mail: kasac@info.bw; **The Flying Mission**, tel: 390 0297, e-mail: charters@flying mission.org and **Mack Air**, in Maun, tel: 686 0675, e-mail: reservations@mackair.co.bw Most hotels offer a bus **shuttle service** to and from the airport 5km (3 miles) north of the city. Within the city the only public transport is **minibus taxis**. **Botswana Railways** runs a daily service to and from Lobatse and Pilane, and a day and overnight train to Francistown, with links to Bulawayo, Harare, Mafikeng and Johannesburg.

## WHERE TO STAY

### Gaborone
#### LUXURY
**Falcon Crest Suites**, tel: 393 5373, e-mail: falconcrest@falconcrest.co.bw Luxury suites with an excellent restaurant in a homely setting. **Gaborone Sun**, tel: 361 6000, e-mail: mb_bw_Reservations @za.suninternational.com Luxury rooms, fine restaurants and a buzzing casino.

**Mondior Gaborone**, tel: 319 0600, e-mail: info@gab. mondior.com Elegant 4-star with spacious rooms and trendy News Café. **Walmont Hotel at the Grand Palm**, tel: 363 7777, e-mail: info@grandpalm.bw Luxury hotel with excellent restaurants, casino and the Gaborone International Conference Centre (GICC).

#### MID-RANGE
**Cresta Lodge**, Samora Machel Drive, tel: 397 5375, e-mail: reslodge@cresta.co.bw Comfortable select services hotel in garden setting with the popular Chatters Restaurant. **Cresta President Hotel**, Main Mall, tel: 395 3631, fax: 395 1840, e-mail: respresident@ cresta.co.bw Ideal business hotel with conference facilities in the heart of the Main Mall. **Metcourt Inn at the Grand Palm**, tel: 363 7907, fax: 391 0402, e-mail: metres@grand palm.bw Access to Walmont facilities.

#### BUDGET
**The Big Five Lodge**, tel: 350 0500, fax: 350 0555. Comfortable thatched chalets, a large swimming pool, restaurant and bar. **Gaborone Hotel and Casino**, tel: 392 2777, fax: 392 2727, e-mail: gh@info.bw Located next to shops, but can be noisy. **Planet Lodge**, tel 391 0116 or 390 3295, e-mail: planet lodge@mega.bw Two good-

value establishments on Bokaa Rd and Southring Rd.

### Kanye
*BUDGET*
**Motse Lodge & Cultural Village**, tel: 548 0363, fax: 548 0370, e-mail: motse lodge@botsnet.bw Luxury chalets and camping.

### Lobatse
*MID-RANGE*
**Cumberland Hotel**, tel: 533 0281, fax: 533 2106, e-mail: enquiries@cumberlandhotel. co.bw Comfortable hotel with casino, pool and good restaurants.

### Phakalane
*LUXURY*
**Phakalane Golf Estate Hotel Resort**, in Phakalane Golf Estate, tel: 393 0000, fax: 315 9663, e-mail: sales@phakalane. co.bw Luxury rooms; the ultimate golfing experience.

## WHERE TO EAT

There are many restaurants and takeaways in Gaborone – the following is just a small selection. As Botswana is a prime beef producer, the steaks are usually excellent. Most hotels serve good roast carveries and traditional *seswaa* and *pap*.

**25° East**, tel: 370 0235. Very good Asian cuisine with expensive imported wines.
**Ashoka Palace Indian Restaurant**, tel: 316 5452. Indian cuisine in the African Mall.
**Bull and Bush**, tel: 397 5070. Famous steakhouse and pub.
**Caravela Portuguese Restaurant**, tel: 391 4284. Long-established favourite.
**Drotsky's**, Phakalane Golf Club, tel: 393 0000. Fine cuisine and outstanding wines.
**The Falconry**, tel: 393 5373. Outstanding cuisine at the Falcon Crest Lodge.
**Moghul Restaurant**, tel: 397 5246. Established Indian, Pakistani and Chinese food.
**Primi-Piatti**, Riverwalk Mall, tel: 370 0068. Great Italian-themed restaurant.
**Rodizio**, tel: 392 4428/9. Brazilian-themed restaurant offering 'eat as much as you can' beef.
**Sanitas Garden Centre**, tel: 395 2538. Wholesome meals served in the nursery garden; playground for the children.
**The No1 Ladies' Opera House**, tel: 316 5459. A small but fascinating Mma Ramotswe-themed theatre and restaurant at 'Kgale Siding'. An experience not to be missed.

## TOURS AND EXCURSIONS

**Arne's Horse Safaris and Retreat**, tel: 390 9091, e-mail: arnesoderstrom@ yahoo.com Accommodation and horse trails in the hills of Kopong north of Gaborone.
**Lion Park Resort**, tel: 7329 3000, e-mail: info@lionpark. co.bw Waterslides, rides and swimming pools.
**Mokolodi Nature Reserve**, tel: 316 1955, fax: 316 5488, e-mail: information@ mokolodi.com or bookings @mokolodi.com The reserve offers rhino and giraffe tracking, elephant-back safaris, game drives, bush braais, more.
**Gaborone Game Reserve**, tel: 318 4492. Excellent bird and game viewing.

## USEFUL CONTACTS

**Department of Surveys and Mapping**, tel: 395 3251 Stockists of maps.
**Botswana Society**, tel: 391 9745. Botswana history and conservation.
**Wildlife and National Parks**, tel: 397 1405.
**Parks & Reserves Reservations**, tel: 318 0774.
**Botswana Tourism Board**, tel: 391 3111.
**Kalahari Conservation Society**, tel: 397 4557.
**Gaborone Private Hospital**, tel: 368 5600.
**Bokamoso Private Hospital**, Mmopane, tel: 369 4000.
**Med Rescue International**, tel: 390 3066 or 686 4455; or **Netcare 911**, tel: 390 4537. Medical rescue and evacuation.

| GABORONE | J | F | M | A | M | J | J | A | S | O | N | D |
|---|---|---|---|---|---|---|---|---|---|---|---|---|
| MIN AVE TEMP. °C | 20 | 19 | 17 | 13 | 8 | 5 | 4 | 7 | 12 | 16 | 18 | 19 |
| MIN AVE TEMP. °F | 68 | 66 | 63 | 55 | 46 | 41 | 39 | 45 | 54 | 61 | 65 | 66 |
| MAX AVE TEMP. °C | 33 | 32 | 30 | 27 | 25 | 22 | 23 | 26 | 29 | 31 | 32 | 32 |
| MAX AVE TEMP. °F | 91 | 90 | 86 | 81 | 77 | 72 | 73 | 79 | 84 | 88 | 90 | 90 |
| RAINFALL mm | 104 | 86 | 58 | 50 | 11 | 4 | 4 | 4 | 17 | 46 | 75 | 73 |
| RAINFALL in | 4.1 | 3.4 | 2.3 | 2 | 0.4 | 0.2 | 0.2 | 0.2 | 0.7 | 1.8 | 3 | 2.9 |

# 3
# The Southern Kalahari

The Kalahari is a vast semidesert which, unlike true deserts, does receive erratic rainfall. It remains, however, a harsh and inhospitable place. There is sufficient vegetation and grass cover to sustain considerable wildlife populations, but the lack of water has forced nature to adapt, and in this fascinating and remote corner of the country visitors find a unique ecology perfectly adapted to the challenging climate. Mankind is, however, less adaptable and, apart from the nomadic San, the region has remained untouched.

## THE KGALAGADI TRANSFRONTIER PARK ★★★

The Gemsbok National Park was the first national park to be established in Botswana back in 1937 to protect the fragile environment and the large herds of wildlife that roamed the area. In 2000 this park was amalgamated with the Kalahari Gemsbok National Park on the South African side to form Africa's first formally declared transborder conservation area – the Kgalagadi Transfrontier Park (KTP). This new park now covers a combined area of about 38,000km² (14,670 sq miles), three quarters of which is in Botswana. There are three main areas of attraction: Mabuasehube, the Wilderness Trails and Two Rivers.

### The Mabuasehube Area ★★★

In 1995 Mabuasehube Game Reserve, with its network of roads and camping facilities was amalgamated into the Gemsbok National Park. This Mabuasehube area

## DON'T MISS

★★★ **Western Woodlands:** camp in an idyllic natural woodland in a remote uninhabited region.
★★★ Finding **cheetah** at the kill.
★★ Watching **leopard** stalking across the open pans.
★★ **Nossob River Valley:** exciting drives.
★ The rare **brown hyena**.
★ **Bat-eared foxes** coming out to play in the evening.
★ The herds of **gemsbok**.

◀ *Opposite: The massive rapier-horned gemsbok (Oryx gazella) is perfectly adapted to the harsh Kalahari environment.*

**45**

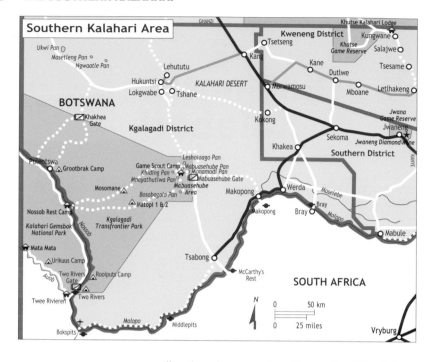

**Southern Kalahari Area**

offers the adventurous traveller a truly wild safari experience. It is from here that two of the five four-by-four trails that cut across this great wilderness start, winding their way across 150km (90 miles) of parched lands to Nossob camp and back.

### The Pans

There are numerous **pans** with camping facilities within 20km (12 miles) north, west and south of the gate. The southernmost pan is **Bosobogolo**, from where the four-by-four 'Matopi' route to Nossob turns away to the west. There are two camp sites along this long, 170km (100-mile) trail. As with almost all the camping sites on the Botswana side of the park, these camp sites have no running water (so bring plenty) and just have pit latrines for self-sufficient campers.

In the middle of the Mabuasehube area is **Mpaya-**

thutwa **Pan** which is known for its leopards. It has a water hole which attracts a great deal of game, especially in the dry winter months. Northwest of Mpayathutwa is **Khiding Pan**. Another 9km (6 miles) further on is the Malatso camp site. It is from here that the 155km (93-mile) one-way four-by-four trail heads out for Nossob. Remember, this is one way only and you have to return either via Two Rivers or to Bosobogolo.

### The Wilderness Trails ★★★

The other three four-by-four trails all leave from the Kaa entrance gate on the northern edge of the park. They are the **Kaa Game Viewing trail**, which meanders in a broad loop for almost 200km (120 miles) around the far north-western corner of the park, the 85km (51-mile) **Kaa to Kannaguass trail**, and the very long looped **Polentswa Wilderness** four-by-four trail, which is a one-way trail that extends 260km (156 miles) from Kaa to the Nossob and back through some of the most challenging and remote country to be found anywhere in the world.

On these trails you are more than likely to see the Transfrontier Park's many 'big cats'. At a recent count, it was estimated that the **Kgalagadi Transfrontier Park** has more than 800 lions, leopards and cheetah.

### Two Rivers ★★★

This portion of the park is extremely remote and is a vast expanse of harsh sandveld that lies along the far southwestern edge of Botswana down to the South African border in the heart of the transfrontier park. The public camp site near the Two Rivers entrance gate, which faces the Twee Rivieren Rest Camp on the South African side of the border, has the luxury of hot showers and flush toilets. From this camp site the border road runs up the length of the Nossob Valley. About 25km (15

▼ Below: There are numerous ostrich farms in the Ghanzi and Kgalagadi Districts.

*▲ Above: Campers enjoy the cool Kalahari desert air as the day draws to a close.*

*▶ Opposite: The pods of the camel thorn tree (Acacia erioloba). The name is a corruption of the Afrikaans, meaning 'giraffe thorn'.*

miles) up this road is the rustic Rooiputs camping ground, and 225km (140 miles) further the Grootbrak and Polentswa camping grounds. Polentswa, which is a starting point for the Wilderness Trail to Kaa, has a very pleasant setting and a good concentration of resident wildlife. But there is no drinking water, so be sure to bring plenty.

### Routes to the Kgalagadi Transfrontier Park

The park is designed for self-sufficient, self-drive visitors. There are three points of entry – Mabuasehube, Kaa and Two Rivers on the South African border. The most common route into Mabuasehube is via Tsabong. Tsabong is 540km (335 miles) southwest of Gaborone, it has a camel park and is the last place with reliable supplies of fuel and provisions. At Tsabong the road to Mabuasehube is signposted 'Tshane 240km'. The road is initially gravel but becomes a sandy track requiring four-wheel-drive. The park entrance gate is 116km (72 miles) north of Tsabong.

To reach the Two Rivers gate, continue another 310km (192 miles) west along a gravel road from Tsabong. It goes via Bokspits and the spectacular red dunes of that far-away corner of the country. Two Rivers is 53km (33 miles) north of Bokspits. Fuel and provisions are available on the South African side of Two Rivers so be sure to have your passports.

Getting to the Kaa entrance gate is a lot more challenging. Take the Trans Kalahari Highway to Kang where you turn off to Hukuntsi. From Hukuntsi drive approximately 85km (50 miles) along the Ncojane road, looking out for a track that goes straight due southwest for about 70km (45 miles) before reaching the park fence. Turn right and Kaa is 6km (4 miles) to the northwest.

## WHEEL WARY

When driving in the park you must be sure to reduce the tyre pressure of your vehicle. This will give you better traction in the sand and reduces the corrugating effect on the roads. As you will need to reinflate your tyres upon reaching the tar road on your way out, it is advisable to carry at least a portable foot pump.

### Jwana Game Park ★★★

Jwana Game Park is a small 20,000-hectare (49,500-acre) conservation area. Prior to its establishment, it was part of the fenced mine lease area surrounding Jwaneng Diamond Mine, but is now home to a wide range of indigenous and re-introduced wildlife, including a couple of white rhino and large herds of red hartebeest, wildebeest, eland, kudu, giraffe and gemsbok. Caracal, leopard and cheetah also roam the scrubland, and a Cheetah Conservation Botswana (CCB) field unit operates in the park studying these endangered cats.

As the park is owned and operated by Debswana as part of the Jwaneng Mine lease area, visitors must have their own vehicles and, although permits are not required, they must register with mine security at the main gate. Arrangements can also be made with the Park Manager on tel: 588 4363 or 7133 6041.

### GHANZI

Ghanzi, known as the 'Capital of the Kalahari', is more the capital of cattle country, as with its fine grazing and abundant groundwater it is reputed to be the best beef range in the world. Although it has never been a tourist destination, in Ghanzi you will find **Ghanzi Craft** which is an outlet and training centre for San craftspeople who sell outstanding works at a fraction of the city prices.

Situated 37km (23 miles) from Ghanzi on the Maun road is the tiny village of **D'Kar** where you will also find the Kuru Museum and Cultural Centre which is definitely worth visiting.

### THE WESTERN WOODLANDS ★★

This vast almost totally uninhabited area along the southwestern edge of Botswana is one of the least known in southern Africa. Here, a remarkable cluster of mature **camel thorn trees** (Acacia erioloba) is set in golden grasslands spreading over an area of about 160km² (60 sq miles) in a

## DESERT SUSTENANCE

The most important plant in the Kgalagadi Transfrontier Park is the **tsamma melon** (Citrullus lanatus) which, in conjunction with the **gemsbok cucumber** (Acathosicyos naudinianus), provides not only a vital source of water for humans, but also a food source for almost all of the animals which inhabit the dunes. The larger mammals also gain important minerals from the salty clays found on the pans. In certain areas these 'game licks' have evolved into pitted and cratered cliffs which are regularly gnawed by the animals. Some of these holes are large enough to accommodate a fully grown man.

# THE SOUTHERN KALAHARI

THE JEWELS OF JWANENG

Jwaneng is a new town north-west of Gaborone. Before 1980 the area consisted of only a few cattleposts, but is now home to over 15,000 people. The town was built in the early 1980s to house employees of Jwaneng mine after diamonds were discovered there in 1976. There is a large multicored kimberlitic pipe at Jwaneng, making this young but rapidly growing mine one of the richest in the world. The open-cast mine pit at Jwaneng is much larger than the famous 'Big Hole' in Kimberley.

## THE CUTLINE GRID

In the 1970s and '80s De Beers did a lot of diamond prospecting in the south and western areas of Botswana including the Kgalagadi Trans-frontier Park. With graders they cut a chequered grid of north–south and east–west tracks across the country, each at roughly 15km (9-mile) intervals. Many of these lines are now overgrown, but others are kept open as roads. If while driving through the Kgalagadi Transfrontier Park you notice that the road is perfectly straight, you are probably driving on one of these old prospecting cutlines.

strip almost 40km (24 miles) long. With virtually no undergrowth the impression given is that of a vast carefully tended park offering numerous idyllic camp sites.

As this area is not in a national park, booking and registration are not required. However, it is one of the planet's last pristine wildernesses, so take care of it.

### Routes to the Woodlands

There are few roads, and those to be found are little more than undefined tracks. There are hardly any supply points, except for fuel and basic commodities at Hukuntsi, so all visitors must be self-sufficient with reserves of water, fuel, a compass, GPS and basic spares in case of a breakdown.

The best route to these remote woodlands is via Kang, where you turn west off the Trans-Kalahari highway to Hukuntsi. From Hukuntsi proceed down the same track to Njocane. Approximately 90km (54 miles) from Hukuntsi lies Masetleng Pan which in the early 1990s was the site of a concerted oil exploration.

The Western Woodlands are approximately 10km (6 miles) northwest of this pan. There is no road to the woodlands and you will have to try the various tracks, but the whole area around Masetleng can be explored and there are other equally inspiring spots waiting to be discovered. The road northwest goes on to the Njocane Farms via Ukwi village and Ukwi Pan, reputed to be the largest pan in Botswana outside of the Makgadikgadi, and eventually on to the Namibian border post at Mamuno.

▶ *Right: After the short rains, Devil's thorn flowers paint the road from Tshane to Mabuasehube.*

## Best Times to Visit

Summers from **September** to **April** are scorching **hot**. The evenings are a bit cooler, but can still be warm. During winter the days are very hot often reaching the 30°C (86°F) mark, but nights can be bitterly cold with heavy frosts and the rare light snowfall. The best times for game viewing in the South African and western Botswana areas are from March to May. In the eastern and Mabuasehube areas the best time to see game is from September to May. But it is extremely hot so try to avoid January to March.

## Getting There

There are airstrips at Tsabong, Twee Rivieren and Nossob Camp. The best route to the Mabuasehube part of the Transfrontier Park is north from Tsabong.

## Getting Around

The park on the Botswana side is only accessible with 4x4s.

## Where to Stay

There are camp sites with barbecues and long-drop toilets at the Mabuaschube pans and along the four-by-four trails.

### CAMPING

Camping at the pans outside the national park is permitted, but if it is in a populated area be sure to ask permission from the local chief or headman. Camp sites are available in **Kang**, **Tsabong** and **Ghanzi**.

### Ghanzi

**Kalahari Arms Hotel**, tel: 659 6298, fax: 659 6532. Comfortable rondavels with *en-suite* facilities, restaurant, pool and bar.
**Motswiri Lodge**, tel: 7211 8811. Luxury lodge and camping in the Kanana Wilderness 22km (13 miles) west of Ghanzi.
**Tautona Lodge**, tel: 659 7499, fax: 659 7500, e-mail: tautona_lodge@botsnet.bw Comfortable thatched lodge on its own private game reserve.
**Dqae Qare San Lodge**, tel: 7252 7321. A unique destination where you can learn the secrets of the Ncoakhoe people who live in the heart of the Kalahari.

### Hukuntsi

**Entabeni Guesthouse**, tel: 651 0075. Budget accommodation.

### Jwaneng

**Cezar Hotel,** tel: 588 1090, fax: 588 1052. New 3-star establishment situated on the main road.
**Mokala Lodge**, tel: 588 0835, fax: 588 0839. Comfortable accommodation, good restaurant, bar and casino.

### Kang

**Echo Lodge**, tel: 651 7094. Three-star fully serviced hotel.
**Kalahari Rest Lodge**, tel: 7377 4009. Chalets, restaurant, pool and game drives.
**Kang Ultra-Stop**, tel: 651 7294. Range of accommodation with swimming pool, good restaurant and bar. Booking is essential.

### Tsabong

**Dikukama Guest House**, tel: 654 0414, fax: 654 0415. Air-conditioned *en-suite* rooms.
**Desert Motel**, tel: 654 0020, e-mail: motel@mega.bw Self-catering accommodation 2km (1.2 miles) north of Tsabong.
**Mokha Lodge**, tel: 654 0366. Selected services hotel.

## Where to Eat

Most of the above establishments have restaurant and catering facilities and there is a good restaurant at Twee Rivieren, but otherwise there are no other facilities in the KTP or woodlands area (not even water), so visitors must be totally self-sufficient.

## Tours and Excursions

Most reputable safari operators can tailor specific trips, but there are no regular tours.

| TSABONG | J | F | M | A | M | J | J | A | S | O | N | D |
|---|---|---|---|---|---|---|---|---|---|---|---|---|
| MIN AVE TEMP. °C | 19 | 19 | 17 | 12 | 6 | 4 | 4 | 5 | 9 | 13 | 16 | 18 |
| MIN AVE TEMP. °F | 66 | 66 | 63 | 54 | 43 | 39 | 39 | 41 | 48 | 55 | 61 | 64 |
| MAX AVE TEMP. °C | 35 | 34 | 32 | 28 | 25 | 22 | 22 | 25 | 29 | 31 | 33 | 35 |
| MAX AVE TEMP. °F | 95 | 93 | 90 | 82 | 77 | 72 | 72 | 77 | 84 | 88 | 91 | 95 |
| RAINFALL mm | 53 | 59 | 51 | 37 | 12 | 4 | 1 | 3 | 5 | 21 | 33 | 33 |
| RAINFALL in | 2.1 | 2.3 | 2 | 1.5 | 0.5 | 0.2 | 0 | 0.1 | 0.2 | 0.8 | 1.3 | 1.3 |

# 4
# The Makgadikgadi Pans

In this modern world of cities and overpopulation, it is almost impossible to imagine a place of wide open, uninhabited spaces under an endless canopy of blue sky.

The Makgadikgadi is such a place. The largest salt pan in the world, its silver-grey surface covers over 12,000km² (7500 sq miles) of completely barren flatness, an area almost the size of Portugal.

This vast complex is all that remains of the super-lake that once covered much of northern Botswana. Thousands of years ago the courses of the Chobe and Zambezi rivers were diverted from the lake and, as it shrank, so the water's salinity increased. All that was left was the sun-baked bed. Today, it is at the Makgadikgadi that visitors find the true peace and serenity of complete isolation.

It is possible that there are still remote areas left to be discovered, while other areas have been occupied for thousands of years, rich with the remains of pre-historic settlements. Vast migrating herds of animals traverse the area and in the wet season thousands of water birds flock to the pans.

There are numerous pans in the Makgadikgadi, but the three major pans are: **Ntwetwe Pan** south of Gweta, the largest pan in the system; **Sua Pan** southwest of Nata; and **Nxai Pan** north of the main Gweta/Maun road.

There are few serviced facilities in the Makgadikgadi and, although there are landing strips at both Gweta and Nata, it is an area more suited to self-sufficient 4WD parties. To reach these remote areas most people will pass through Francistown, the gateway to northern Botswana.

## DON'T MISS

★★★ Being surrounded by **flamingoes** in a sea of pink.
★★★ **Sua Pan:** a 4WD cruise under a full moon.
★★★ **Kubu Island:** witness a golden sunrise.
★★ Watching massive herds of **migrating zebra**.
★★ **Baines' Baobabs:** spectacular after rainfall.
★★ Speeding across the pans on a quad-bike.
★ Discovering the signatures of old explorers on ancient **baobab trees**.

◄ *Opposite: The shallow water of the rain-filled Makgadikgadi reflects an expansive sky.*

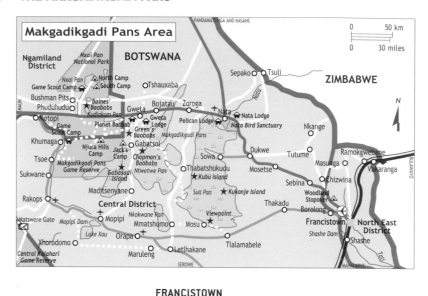

Makgadikgadi Pans Area

### FRANCISTOWN

As one of the oldest towns in Botswana and site of southern Africa's first gold rush, Francistown has grown fast and is now home to 150,000 people. It has managed to retain its 'frontier town' character despite being Botswana's second-largest urban centre and '**Capital of the North**'.

Evidence of human habitation goes back for 80,000 years, but it was only in the 1860s when the geologist **Karl Mauch** discovered **gold** at Tati that the town was established. Soon after the initial discoveries at Tati, more gold deposits were discovered at Francistown. Prospectors rushed into the area from as far away as Australia expecting Francistown to be the Ophir of Africa.

The town was named after **Daniel Francis** who came to Tati in the 1860s and organized the establishment of the town through the sale of freehold stands to the public.

Initially the town consisted of just one main street running parallel to the 'Cape to Cairo' railway along which there were numerous bustling stores and rowdy saloons. Many reminders of this bygone era are preserved in the evocative mine names which remain, such as 'Bonanza', 'Jim's Luck', 'Lady Mary', 'Phoenix', and 'White Elephant'.

### CLIMATE

The Makgadikgadi is very hot in the summer months from October to May, relieved by infrequent showers and thunderstorms. If there is water in the pans they can become uncomfortably humid with the high level of evaporation. In winter, from June to September, the days are warm but the nights can be bitterly cold with temperatures dropping to well below freezing. In October the area is prone to windstorms and can be very dusty.

◀ *Left: The busy, shop-lined Blue Jacket Street which runs through the middle of Francistown.*

## BLUE JACKET

'Blue Jacket' is the name of not only a mine, but also the main street running through Francistown. It is in memory of an old prospector, Sam Andersen, who had become famous (before arriving in Botswana) as the first man to cross the western desert in Australia on foot with his prospecting wheelbarrow. The name 'Blue Jacket' came into existence because of Sam's habit of always wearing a blue denim jacket wherever he went.

The gold in eastern Botswana is a complex mix of narrow reefs, difficult for early miners to extract; by the 1940s much of the small-scale mining had ceased. Today, there is little in the way of gold mining in Francistown, although a mine recently established west of the city has brought new life to the local industry.

Located at the head of the railway line and the junction of the Maun/Kasane and Bulawayo roads, Francistown has been a natural growth point. Over the last few years the city has grown rapidly to cater for the needs of Zimbabweans across the border and now boasts numerous shopping centres and wholesalers. There are also several good hotels, a couple of casinos, shopping malls, nightclubs, one of the largest referral hospitals in Botswana, a library, well-kept parks, and colourful markets, which, combined with the town's friendly reputation, makes it a pleasant and comfortable stopover.

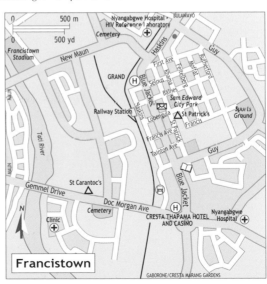

# THE MAKGADIKGADI PANS

## THE PYRAMIDS

The 'pyramids' are a collo-quial name given by the writer Mike Main to a collection of spoil dumps next to an exploratory trench in the northern tip of Sua Pan west of Nata. Due to the high **salinity** of the water one has incredible buoyancy when swimming in the trench, but the real fascination is the strange lifeforms which grow in the water. These blue-green knots of **algae** have been iden-tified as original stramatolites, the earliest lifeforms known to man and which appear to have remained unchanged for over 2.5 billion years. The presence of this lifeform is a very unusual phenomenon, so treat the site with respect.

## Museum Supa-Ngwao **

The Museum Supa-Ngwao is the cultural centre of north-eastern Botswana with exhibits depicting the heritage of the local people and the history of Francistown itself. There is also a tourist information centre and a craft shop at the museum, located near the central ring road. Open 08:00–13:00 and 14:00–17:00 Monday–Friday, 09:00–17:00 Saturday; tel: 240 3088, e-mail: <u>snm@info.bw</u>

## NORTH OF FRANCISTOWN

The village of Nata lies 187km (113 miles) from Francistown, but some 15km (9 miles) before this tradi-tional village is the entrance to the Nata Sanctuary.

## Nata Bird Sanctuary ***

Recognized by UNESCO as being one of the largest breeding sites of lesser and greater flamingo in the world, this 230km$^2$ (90-sq-mile) sanctuary was estab-lished in the early 1990s on the northeastern edge of Sua Pan. More than 165 bird species can be seen in the park, along with the quarter million migrant flamingoes that arrive with the rains.

The sanctuary is a local community project managed by a board of trustees selected from the four nearby villages. This unique approach to community involve-ment in ecotourism is considered to be the key to conservation throughout Africa.

During the wet season the Nata River carries water from Zimbabwe into Sua Pan, filling its northern region and attracting a wide variety of water birds. In the dry winter months bustards and korhaans can be seen in the grassy fringes, accompanied by migratory birds such as kites, eagles and bee-eaters.

There are numerous secluded camp sites at the entrance gate and throughout the park, all carefully positioned for both shade and panoramic views across the pre-pan grasslands. The sanctuary is open daily from 07:00 to 19:00.

▶ *Opposite: The picturesque village of Nata near the edge of the Makgadikgadi.*
▼ *Below: A flotilla of pelicans fishing in the shallows of the Nata Bird Sanctuary.*

While the roads throughout the sanctuary are well maintained, access to certain areas may be restricted to four-wheel-drive, particularly in the wet season when the black cotton soil can be treacherous.

### Nata Village **

This traditional village, set on the Nata River banks, is very scenic, with decorated huts and administrative buildings in a grove of Ilala palms.

There are now numerous accommodation options in and around Nata, from the long-established Nata Lodge to the newer Northgate and Pelican lodges, all of which offer excursions, quad-bike trails and sunset cruises onto the pans and to the Bird Sanctuary. Nata and Pelican lodges have well-serviced camp sites, and there is a public camp site on the banks of the Nata River 3km (2 miles) upstream from the village.

### The Pans ***

There are numerous pans in the Makgadikgadi, but the three main ones are Ntwetwe Pan, Sua Pan and the smaller Nxai Pan north of the A3 highway. Nata is at the northern tip of Sua Pan.

### SUA PAN ***

Sua (or Sowa) is the San word for salt, an apt description of this vast white expanse.

## THE PINK TIDE

Every year after the rains, when the eastern edge of Sua Pan fills with water, the 'Pink Tide' comes in. Thousands of greater and lesser **flamingos** (*Phoenicopterus ruber* and *Phoenicopterus minor*) flock to the pans which are the largest breeding site for greater flamingos in Africa. The greater flamingos feed on brine shrimps, worms and crustaceans and nest on islands, while the lesser flamingos feed on algae and build tall mud-cone nests on the pan surface, just as the water is receding. These cones protect the chicks from the severe heat. The heat is, however, not the only hazard they face; before the young birds are able to fly the water dries up, forcing their parents to walk them sometimes as far as 150km (90 miles) to the last of the water in northern Sua. Many of the babies die on the way, but this strange cycle is endlessly repeated.

### SUA'S SODA ASH

Just beneath the surface of Sua Pan are vast quantities of **soda ash**, used in the manufacture of glass, ceramics, soap and paper as well as being a useful cleaning agent. With the obvious economic potential of this natural resource, in the early 1990s a new town was built on the **Sua Spit** to service a massive mining operation on the pan. The plant included the construction of 55 wells in a wellfield covering 200km² (125 sq miles). The project was, however, placed in provisional liquidation in 1995. New investors relaunched the operation under the name **Botash**. This preserved many jobs, but with dropping international prices and unfavourable exchange rates Botash is unlikely to be the economic booster it was hoped to be.

▼ *Below: In years of good rain Sua Pan attracts hundreds of thousands of greater and lesser flamingoes.*

Most visitors only access the eastern edge of Sua Pan, with short forays onto the outstretched surface from Nata village or the Bird Sanctuary, but it is a vast area with several days being required to fully appreciate it.

There are very few rock islands in the Makgadikgadi, but in southern Sua a scattering of granite isles lie on the white surface like beached whales. All have unique characteristics that give this desolate place its mesmeric attraction. Of all the islands, Kubu (which means 'hippo' in Setswana) is the most famous.

### Kubu Island ★★★

Rising no more than 20m (70ft) above the pan, this national monument, with its fossil beaches, stunted baobab trees and mysterious stone walls, leaves an indelible impression upon all who visit its water-worn shores. Many of Kubu's rocks are stained white with fossilized bird droppings. This ancient guano is called apatite and bears testimony to a large bird population that used to live on the island, feeding off the fish of the waters that surrounded their rocky knoll.

There is a trig-beacon on the island's summit. The rocks on the northeastern side are all smoothed by wave action, while on the opposite leeward side are thousands of small, rounded pebbles, which used to protrude as a tiny wave-washed beach. As the level of this immense inland sea rose and fell, there were times when Kubu was deep beneath the waves, others when it lay exposed in a sea of sand and others when it hardly showed above the surface, surrounded by 100km (60 miles) of sea.

There are no camping facilities on Kubu or the other islands of southwestern Sua, but there are many idyllic spots overlooking the pan. Campers must bring their own firewood and must remove all their litter. A further 38km (24 miles) to the east lies the seldom-visited **Kukonje Island**.

### Routes to Kubu Island

There are several routes to Kubu, all requiring four-wheel-drive, but most travel agents or tour operators can organize special trips to Kubu for those without.

The easiest route to Kubu is from Francistown. Take the Orapa road from Francistown and continue for 200km (125 miles) until you reach a dirt road which intersects with the main road. There is a sign indicating Letlhakane to the left. At the crossroads take the road to the right, to the village of Mmatshumo.

▲ Above: The stunted, salt-stained baobabs of Kubu guard the island's rocky beaches.

Drive through the village, keeping to the main northern track. This is the track to the pans, Thabatshukudu village and eventually the Nata/Maun road. A short distance beyond Mmatshumo the road descends the escarpment giving a breaktaking view of the pan. Approximately 26km (16 miles) out of Mmatshumo is an unmarked track to the right. Take this turn-off and Kubu is 18km (11 miles) further on. For those with GPS the co-ordinates are 20°53'50" S latitude and 25°49'41" E longitude.

The ruined stone wall on Kubu encloses what appears to have been an uninhabited area. Archaeologists consider it to have been a ritualistic initiation site.

There is much greater evidence of ancient human habitation near the village of Mosu, south of Kubu Island.

### Mosu *

This scenic palm-lined village overlooks the sprawling pan from the edge of a 40m (130ft) escarpment. It is here that one of Botswana's greatest **archaeological sites** has been discovered.

It is an extremely remote and inaccessible place but, for the historically inclined, it is an amazing area where new discoveries can be made around almost every corner. Virtually every headland overlooking the pan, or sea as it was, on the shores of southern Sua is the site of an ancient settlement.

## ARCHAEOLOGIST'S PARADISE

There has been little archaeological research in northern Botswana but there are countless sites of interest around the Makgadikgadi, including ancient settlements and rich fossil beds. On the pans you will find Stone Age tools, while fossilized papyrus stems and mollusc shells litter the surrounding areas. In the west near the Boteti River are areas which are scattered with Stone Age tools and hand axes. With the premium for suitable stone, local residents in these regions collect the stones in piles, selling them off for building material. Possibly as many as 10% of the rocks in these piles are actually hand-chipped Stone-Age tools, which are being sold off as cheap building materials.

▲ *Above: A herd of springbok shares a water hole on Nxai Pan with a flock of birds.*
▶ *Opposite: As there are hardly any landmarks in the Makgadikgadi, visitors crossing the pans must be totally self-sufficient.*

### GETTING UNSTUCK

Getting stuck in a pan is a common problem and it can take hours or sometimes days to dig your way out. Even if you have a winch there is nothing to attach it to on the flat featureless pan surface. In this situation, dig a hole to the exact size of your spare wheel 6m (20ft) away and at right angles to the front of your vehicle. Attach the winch to the spare wheel and sink it into the hole. This should provide a suitable anchor for the winch to extract your vehicle.

### Ntwetwe Pan ***

Ntwetwe Pan is the western twin of Sua and is just as large, with its endless white lunar landscape that melts into the blue sky, enveloping visitors in its awesome vastness.

The pan was once watered by the Boteti River, but it is now permanently dry following the construction of the Mopipi Dam that provides water for the diamond mine at Orapa.

One of the few features on the flat surface of the pan is Gabasadi Island, a low mound that can be seen in the middle of Ntwetwe just west of the north/south route across the pan. This is actually an ancient crescent-shaped barchan sand dune. It is an easy climb and offers good views across the pan – and the curvature of the earth.

### Gweta **

The quaint village of Gweta is an established settlement near **Ntwetwe Pan**, 100km (60 miles) from Nata on the main Maun road. It is a dry, dusty spot, but its name, which means 'place of the big frogs', implies a wetter past. In years of exceptional rain, bullfrogs are still reputed to miraculously appear in the village. In Gweta there is a petrol station, a general dealer, a liquor store and a couple of comfortable and inexpensive lodges.

### Planet Baobab **

Reputed to be the 'funkiest camp in the entire Kalahari', Planet Baobab is a unique array of traditionally styled *en-suite* Bakalanga huts. The thick-walled and shaggy thatched huts have been built in a stand of baobab trees and serviced with a huge round swimming pool, a bar and a restaurant serving real African cuisine. Planet Baobab is certainly an unforgettable experience.

## THE MAKGADIKGADI AND NXAI PAN NATIONAL PARK ***

This national park covers approximately 7500km² (2850 sq miles), extending across both sides of the main Gweta/Maun road. The national park includes several large pans with a selection of camping sites, but one of its biggest attractions is the famous 'Baines' Baobabs'.

Four-wheel-drive is recommended throughout this area, as even in the dry season the pan surface can be treacherous with the unseen water table lurking often just inches under the hard-baked surface. Once on the pans the exhilaration of speeding across the flat surface is unforgettable.

While there are no fixed lodges or hotels in the park, there are several designated camp sites. This limits access to all but fully equipped self-drive visitors, or those on tailor-made safaris.

### Xhumaga Camp Site *

In the southern section of the park there are two camp sites. One is at Xhumaga overlooking the Boteti River and Hippo Pool No. 1 near the Game Scout Camp on the extreme western edge of the park. At this camp site is an observation platform overlooking the river and a grove of acacia trees providing good shade even in the height of summer. There is an ablution block with running borehole water and cold showers. Visitors should bring their own firewood or use gas cookers.

### SAN PITS

Near the village of Phuduhudu there are numerous hand-dug holes and wells. These were dug by the San not only for water but also as hides from which they could ambush passing game with poison-tipped arrows. Take the old gravel Nata/Maun road west from Phuduhudu for about 10km (6 miles) and you'll find the sprawled ruins of an old cattlepost under a collection of huge shady trees. The pits are in the immediate vicinity. Zebra and wildebeest often rest under the trees on their way to and from the pans.

### Njuca Camp Site *

The second camp site is near the east of the park, 40km (24 miles) from Xhumaga and 20km (12 miles) from the Game Scout Camp on the low Njuca hills. In most places these 'hills' would be little more than unnamed undulations, but on the perfectly level Makgadikgadi their slight elevation affords incredible

### THE UPSIDE-DOWN TREE

The baobab *(Adansonia digitata)* tree can grow to over 40m (130ft) in diameter. There are countless legends about the baobab; the San believe that there are no young baobabs, but that God throws fully grown ones down from heaven. Unfortunately being top-heavy they always land with their roots in the air. Another is that the hyena is responsible for its appearance. When God planted trees on earth he gave one to each animal. The hyena was last in line and was left with the strange-looking baobab. In disgust he pulled it out of the ground and replanted it upside down! Reputed to grow up to 4000 years old, these giants have numerous nutritional and medicinal properties. Their leaves are rich in vitamin C and they store incredible volumes of water both in their wood and in hollows in their trunks.

views of up to 15km (9 miles) across the shimmering pan. There are pit latrines at Njuca, but **no water**.

### THE BAOBAB TRAIL

With the almost total absence of landmarks in the Makgadikgadi, the huge baobab trees which grow there became points of navigation for early explorers. This is strange considering that baobabs are technically not trees at all, but the world's largest giant succulents. Around the pans, almost every baobab can tell a story through the old signatures carved on it.

On the northern edge of Ntwetwe near Gutsha Pan is **Green's Baobab**, which bears not only the signatures of 'Green's Expedition' dated 1858–1859, but also an elusive 'H V Z – 1851/2', which some consider could have been carved by the flamboyant Hendrick Van Zyl, founder of the town of Ghanzi.

Some 9km (5 miles) south from Green's Baobab is another monster, 'Chapman's Baobab', visible from up to 20km (12 miles) away, which entices the imagination with a gothic 'J C'. However, these are the initials of James Chapman who passed this way with the painter Thomas Baines in 1862. In the middle of the spreading trunk of this great tree is a hollow recess which was used as a post box by many early travellers, a habit which led to this meeting place becoming known as the Post Office Tree. More famous than these trees, however, are Baines' Baobabs.

Both Baines' Baobabs and Kudiakam Pan, over which they look, are in the northern section of the

Makgadikgadi Pans Game Reserve. There is only one track into this part of the reserve which turns off the Nata/Maun road 77km (46 miles) from Gweta and 135km (81 miles) before Maun.

The sandy track is only navigable by four-wheel-drive. After 15km (9 miles) there is a cross road, which is the original Nata/Maun road. A left turn takes you to the village of **Phuduhudu**, while right takes you to Baines' Baobabs. Continue straight to reach the Game Scout Camp which is a further 18km (11 miles) along this track. Just beyond the entrance gate the road winds up a series of sand dunes. The dunes' summit rises about 20m (65ft) above the plain and it is from here that one is

greeted by the first view across the expanse of Nxai Pan.

▲ *Above: Blue wildebeest gather in the grassy woodlands for their annual migration.*
◀ *Opposite: Baines' Baobabs stand much as they did when the famous painter and naturalist Thomas Baines paid an historic visit to the area.*

### Baines' Baobabs ***

This remarkable cluster of trees, also known as the Seven Sisters, has been immortalized by photographers and painters over the years, including Prince Charles, but they were made famous by the painter and naturalist Thomas Baines who was the first to paint them during his expedition in 1862. Since this watercolour was done well over 140 years ago the scene has hardly changed except, sadly, for the growing amount of litter.

The seven giant trees dominate a small island on the edge of the open grassless Kudiakam Pan. They create an ideal picnic spot and always afford visitors respite in their deep, cool shade.

People often used to camp here, but now that this area has been incorporated in the national park this is no longer permitted, and it will be years before the area recovers from the damage of uncontrolled camping.

To get to Baines' Baobabs, take the western turning at the Phuduhudu crossroads. At 11km (7 miles), the dry route, which veers to the right, is the shorter and more attractive of the two routes, taking you along Kudiakam Pan to the baobabs. If the ground is wet or if there has been recent rain, take the left route, which goes for just over 13km (8 miles) before you will see the trees on the right. Take the right turn and go for a further 3.5km (2 miles) along this track until you reach the landmark.

### WILDEBEEST ON THE MOVE

Blue wildebeest, which are now by no means the most common antelope in the area, were once plentiful. In 1980 the last huge migration of these animals, reminiscent of the vast Serengeti migrations, crossed the Makgadikgadi. Over 100,000 animals were involved and the herd was over 16km (10 miles) long and 10km (6 miles) wide.

### NXAI PAN ★★★

Unlike the salt pans which characterize the rest of the Makgadikgadi, Nxai Pan is covered with short sweet grass which provides good grazing and attracts large herds of springbok and impala. It is very unusual to see these two antelope species together on the same range and the only other place where this occurs to a significant degree is Etosha Pan in Namibia. Other game includes the desert-adapted gemsbok, giraffe, kudu, hartebeest, zebra, and the migratory wildebeest, as well as leopard, lion and hyena.

### South Camp ★

There are two camp sites at Nxai Pan. South Camp is a short distance from the Scout Camp on the edge of Nxai. Take a right turn directly after entering the old gate; the camp is set in a grove of terminalia trees. There is an observation platform from which one can view game including (if you are lucky) leopard.

There is a remarkable array of birds to be seen in the Nxai Pan area, including the very common black korhaan, kestrels and goshawks, as well as the world's heaviest flying bird, the kori bustard which weighs in at nearly 40kg (88lb).

▼ *Below: A Kalahari tent tortoise, knee-high in water, illustrates the miniscule depth of the rain-filled pan.*

### North Camp ★

North Camp is at the top end of Nxai Pan, 8km (5 miles) from the old gate. It is set in a clearing in mopane woodland, but does not have a great deal of shade or a view of the pan. Both North and South camps have barbecue sites, running water and ablution blocks with flush toilets and shower facilities.

## Best Times to Visit

The southern Makgadikgadi and Nxai Pan Game Reserve, Ntwetwe and Sua Pans are best for **game viewing** from **Apr–Jul**. In the Nxai Pan area, game viewing is best from **Dec–Apr**. In eastern Sua, **water birds** can be seen between **Jan–Mar** depending on the rains and the flow of the Nata River. Roads can become impassable during the wet season (Dec–Mar). There can be violent **dust storms** in **October** and early **November**.

## Getting There

There are airstrips at Gweta and Nata. Four wheel drive is necessary in the park. Hitch-hiking is not advisable. There is a good tar road from Francistown and Maun. Vehicles can be hired from Maun and Francistown where there are larger airports.

## Getting Around

Four-wheel-drive is vital. Tell someone your itinerary so they can organize a search if you break down. Also consider hiring a guide.

## Where to Stay

*Luxury*
**Jack's Camp**, tel: +27 11 447 1605. Luxurious 1940s-style camp; 2012 Condé Nast Gold List winner.
**San Camp**, tel: +27 11 447 1605. Luxury in a palm grove on the edge of the endless pan.

*Mid-range and Budget*
**Nata Lodge**, between Nata and Bird Sanctuary, tel: 620

0070/2. Very comfortable chalets, camping, restaurant, pool and pan trips.
**Pelican Lodge**, tel: 7131 4603. Thatched chalets and gorgeous vistas.
**Gweta Lodge**, in Gweta village near Ntwetwe Pan, tel: 621 2220, fax: 621 2458. Chalets, camp sites.
**Planet Boabab**, tel: 7233 8344. Traditional cultural village.
**National Park camp sites**, book through Parks and Reserves. Reservations, tel: 318 0774, fax: 318 0775.

*Francistown*
*Luxury*
**Cresta Thapama**, tel: 241 3872, e-mail: resthapama@cresta.co.bw Luxury accommodation, restaurant and casino.
**Cresta Marang Gardens**, tel: 241 3991, e-mail: resmarang@cresta.co.bw Has an excellent à la carte restaurant, and accommodation in luxury rooms and tree-top cabins.

*Mid-range*
**Adansonl Hotel**, tel: 241 9714, fax: 241 9715. Three-star hotel and conference centre.
**Metcourt Lodge**, tel: 244 1100, fax: 244 0775, e-mail:

info@ft.metcourt.com Comfortable new hotel.
**Tati River Lodge**, tel: 240 6000, fax: 240 6080. Three-star fully serviced hotel with good Mophane Grill restaurant.
**Wingate Lodge**, tel: 240 1554. Newly built with restaurant.

*Budget*
**Diggers Inn**, tel: 244 0544. Comfortable accommodation in Village Mall.
**Woodlands Stopover**, tel: 244 0131. Comfortable self-drive accommodation.

## Where to Eat

Visitors to Makgadikgadi must bring their own provisions and water. Supplies can be bought in Francistown, Maun, Nata, Gweta and Serowe. There are good restaurants at the above hotels and lodges.

## Tours and Excursions

**Guided safaris:** safari operators offer horseback safaris, quad-bike excursions and sand windsurfing. If there is water on the pans canoeing and sailing are also possible. Jack's Camp and Gweta Lodge offer quad-bike safaris. Gweta Lodge and Nata Lodge organize horseback safaris.

| NATA | J | F | M | A | M | J | J | A | S | O | N | D |
|---|---|---|---|---|---|---|---|---|---|---|---|---|
| MIN AVE TEMP. °C | 19 | 18 | 17 | 14 | 9 | 6 | 5 | 8 | 12 | 16 | 18 | 19 |
| MIN AVE TEMP. °F | 66 | 64 | 63 | 57 | 48 | 43 | 41 | 46 | 54 | 61 | 64 | 66 |
| MAX AVE TEMP. °C | 31 | 30 | 30 | 28 | 26 | 23 | 23 | 26 | 30 | 31 | 31 | 31 |
| MAX AVE TEMP. °F | 88 | 86 | 86 | 82 | 79 | 73 | 73 | 79 | 86 | 88 | 88 | 88 |
| RAINFALL mm | 111 | 97 | 58 | 29 | 2 | 2 | 1 | 0 | 5 | 29 | 55 | 91 |
| RAINFALL in | 4.4 | 3.8 | 2.3 | 1.1 | 0.1 | 0.1 | 0 | 0 | 0.2 | 1.1 | 2.2 | 3.6 |

# 5
# The Tuli Block and Eastern Botswana

The Kalahari sands don't quite reach the far eastern edge of Botswana and, with a higher average rainfall than elsewhere, this thin strip of land has the greatest agricultural potential in an otherwise barren country. Almost 80% of Botswana's population lives in this region, stretching from Ramokgwebana northeast of Francistown to Ramatlabama southwest of Lobatse. Between these points lie the urban centres of Gaborone, Mahalapye, Palapye, Selebi-Phikwe and Francistown, and the wildlife reserves of the Tuli Block.

## THE TULI BLOCK

Set in a landscape of striking natural beauty in the extreme southeast of the country, the Tuli Block is a thin strip of commercial farmland which includes the largest privately owned game conservation area in southern Africa, combining an area of 120,000ha (300,000 acres) of game reserves, hunting and conservation areas.

The land was originally ceded to the British government by **Chief Khama III** of the Ngwato tribe in 1885. It was intended to establish a buffer zone to halt the Boer expansion and provide the British with a corridor in which to build their planned 'Cape to Cairo' railway line. However, the concession proved unsuitable for the railway, which was eventually built further to the west. The British finally transferred its administration to Cecil Rhodes' British South Africa Company (BSAC) which had colonized Rhodesia. In 1904, the BSAC divided the Tuli Block into lots which it sold to European farmers.

◄ *Opposite: Mashatu boasts the largest elephant population on private land anywhere in the world.*

### Eastern Botswana

Over a period of time, as ownership of these farms began to consolidate and as government pressure increased for better utilization of the land, it became possible for private game reserves to be established. In the 1960s the owners of 35 adjoining farms agreed to pull their fences down to allow the free movement of the wildlife, and so the **Northern Tuli Game Reserve**, which occupies the entire Tuli Block north of the Motloutse River, came into being. This large reserve is made up of several smaller private reserves such as the Mashatu and Tuli game reserves and the Kwa Tuli and Stevensford game reserves to the south.

### GREATER MAPUNGUBWE TRANSFRONTIER CONSERVATION AREA ★★★

In 2006 the governments of Botswana, South Africa and Zimbabwe agreed to incorporate their adjacent conservation areas on either side of the Limpopo and Shashe rivers into one huge 5000km² (1900-sq-mile) reserve, then known as the Shashe/Limpopo Transfrontier Conservation Area (TFCA).

This area, Africa's second international 'Peace Park', has continued to develop. At a ceremony at the confluence of the Limpopo and Shashe rivers in 2009 the three bordering countries agreed to rename the conservation area the Greater Mapungubwe TFCA. It now straddles the eastern corner of Botswana, the southwestern corner of Zimbabwe and the northwestern corner of South Africa.

▲ *Above: Guests enjoy a sumptuous breakfast after an early morning game drive in Mashatu.*

The name Mapungubwe was chosen as there are archeological sites in all three countries near the river confluence with the same name, reflecting their shared cultural heritage. This Mapungubwe World Heritage Site is the home to the famous gold rhino that was the symbol of power of the Mapungubwe tribe whose kingdom spanned this area between AD900 and 1300. At its height this lost civilization is reputed to have traded with Arabia, Egypt, India and even China. Today their memory is preserved in the name of the park where tourists can visit their sparse remains, and wonder ...

This area is extremely rich with astounding natural beauty and diversity: riverine forests, wooded river banks, open grasslands and rocky outcrops, not to mention the wildlife, which includes the world's largest herd of privately owned elephant, lion, leopard and cheetah, and well over 350 different types of birds, including the colourful Meyer's parrot.

One of the reserve's major attractions are the unique game-viewing walks and night drives which are on offer. The latter are not permitted in Botswana's national parks, so many visitors miss seeing the 'mini-kangaroo' springhares and the nocturnal predators such as leopard, lynx and wild cat, which are common sightings in Tuli, as well as the more unusual night creatures, such as the aardvarks and the porcupines.

## THE TULI CIRCLE

South of Francistown the Zimbabwe/Botswana border is defined by the Shashe River, except for a unique semicircle of land called the Tuli Circle that juts into Botswana at the head of the Tuli Block. This piece of land was granted to the British South Africa Company in 1891 by Khama III to ensure that the outbreak of lung sickness did not infect the cattle at Fort Tuli. It is also interesting to note that the 16km (9-mile) radius of the circle is the exact range of the largest artillery gun stationed in the fort at the time!

▲ *Above: Over 1000 years ago the Tuli area was the centre of the Mapungubwe Empire. All that remains are numerous unexcavated ruins.*
▶ *Opposite: The idyllic swimming pool at Tuli Safari Lodge.*

## DUST BUSH DRAGGING

Along the dirt roads on the way to Tuli, motorists are warned to beware of 'dust bush dragging'. The term refers to the local practice of dragging a felled tree or bush along the road to flatten the rough corrugations that have developed due to rain and traffic. It can be most unpleasant to get stuck behind a tractor dragging a tree, and it is very dangerous to overtake it through a solid wall of dust.

## Routes into the Tuli Area

The private lodges in the area all have access to landing strips and many visitors choose to fly in. Although as the main roads into the area are mostly tarred, with only the occasional short section of good gravel, Tuli is also an ideal self-drive destination.

There are two main recommended routes depending on whether you are coming from Botswana or South Africa. Tuli is about 500km (300 miles) from both Gaborone and Johannesburg, although the drive from Johannesburg is quicker and more direct.

From either Gaborone or Francistown the best route is via Bobonong, which is likely to be the last place you will get fuel, so fill up. As you enter the village at the first (and only) traffic circle, turn right. Drive about 1km (0.6 mile) to the T-junction and take the right turn signposted 'Mathathane'. Take the next turning left signposted 'Tuli Farms/Mathathane' and drive for a further 50km (30 miles) before turning left to the signposted village of Motlhabaneng which is 15km (9 miles) away on a good dirt road.

Cross the bridge, stay on the dirt road and follow the yellow signs to Mashatu, which after some 40km (24 miles) will get you to the Limpopo Valley Airfield and the B141 Transit Road through the Talana Farms and the Northern Tuli Game Reserve.

It is important to go via Motlhabaneng as this is the only bridge over the Motloutse River and the other routes involve crossing the river bed, which has very soft sand and sometimes very deep water.

The route from Johannesburg is tar all the way to the Pont Drift border post, and goes via Polokwane (formerly

Pietersburg). From Polokwane take the R521 to Alldays via the villages of Mogwadi and Vivo. Most lodges collect their clients at the border post, although be aware that the border closes at 16:00.

If the Limpopo is in flood you will have to cross the river in the wire cage of the Mashatu Cableway, which is quite an experience in itself!

## MASHATU GAME RESERVE ★★★

Mashatu Game Reserve occupies a fascinating area of history and legend south of the Tuli Circle, covering 25,000ha (62,000 acres) of unspoilt wilderness.

With over 800 elephants, Mashatu boasts the largest elephant population on private land in the world and offers guests accommodation at the famous Mashatu Main Camp, in luxury tents at Mashatu Tent Camp, or at Mashatu River Camp, Rock Camp and the Tented Camp, all of which serve outstanding cuisine.

## NORTHERN TULI GAME RESERVE ★★★
### Tuli Safari Lodge ★★★

The luxurious Tuli Safari Lodge, rebuilt after the disastrous flooding of 2013, is the oldest lodge in the area, idyllically situated on the 72,000ha (180,000-acre) privately owned Northern Tuli Game Reserve.

In the reserve there are three game hides overlooking water holes, one of which offers accommodation for guests who want to experience the true thrill of a wild African night.

## SOLOMON'S WALL AND THE GRANITE HILLS
### Solomon's Wall ★★★

Of all the many fascinating geological features in Botswana, Solomon's Wall in the Tuli Block is one of the most remarkable. This basalt dyke once formed a natural

---

### THE RIVER OF DIAMONDS

The Motloutse River, (the name means 'Great Elephant') can trace its source to the west of Francistown. Eons ago, diamonds were carried along the river course, where they lay until the 1950s when the first diamonds in Botswana were discovered in the Motloutse's river bed near Solomon's Wall. After 12 years of intensive prospecting these diamonds led to the discovery of the Orapa diamond pipe, the second-largest kimberlite pipe in the world.

dam wall across the Motloutse River, and the two sides of this breached barrier still stand up to 30m (100ft) high, guarding each side of the narrow gorge.

The vertical sides of this ancient dyke held back a great lake behind what must have been a beautiful waterfall. Evidence of this lake is in the number of alluvial semiprecious stones that can be found in this area along the Motloutse's river bed.

Four-wheel-drive is necessary to reach Solomon's Wall, but it is well worth visiting. There are often deep pools of water, and shade under the fever trees, but it is private property and you must have permission to visit the site.

In the Tuli area there are also two ranges of granite hills which are of great historical and archaeological interest.

### The Lepokole Hills ★★

The Lepokole Hills north of Bobonong are the southern-most extension of the Matopos Hills in Zimbabwe, and are made up of the same immense granite blocks, often piled high into tall castles of fissured rock.

It is in these hills that the last of the **San** in eastern Botswana took refuge from the encroaching 'civilization'. Their presence is recorded in the paintings found in the caves and rocky overhangs of the *kopjes*. In addition to the San paintings, the Lepokole Hills also contain a wealth of archaeological treasures, from Stone Age tools and ancient pottery to stone walls and mud granaries all left by long-forgotten people.

Visitors to the Lepokole Hills must be completely self-sufficient as only basic supplies can be obtained

▼ *Below: The towering buttress of Solomon's Wall juts into the Motloutse riverbed.*

in Bobonong. From the village a rough four-wheel-drive track leads visitors for 15km (9 miles) into the hills. There are no public camp sites or facilities in the hills and if one wants to camp in the area it is a courtesy to ask permission from the *kgosi* (chief) in Bobonong.

## Tswapong Hills **

For the more adventurous, a true journey of discovery awaits those

▲ *Above: the closest relative to the inquisitive dassie is the elephant.*

who set out to explore the Tswapong Hills east of Palapye. This is probably one of the least known areas of Botswana, yet it is less than 50km (30 miles) off the main Gaborone/Francistown highway.

The sheer-sided hills are made up of compressed layers of sandstone, shales and quartzites, giving them their distinctive colours

It is, however, the water which is Tswapong's unique attraction. In this thirsty country, deep gorges have been carved into the hills giving rise to seasonal rivers, fed by natural springs where absorbed rain flows out of the porous rock. In places, these springs give rise to streams forming waterfalls with deep moss-edged pools.

Several waterfalls can be found near the village of Moremi, while a large colony of **Cape vultures** is established in the cliffs near the village of Gootau. Before visiting either of these sites, be sure to ask permission from the village chiefs.

With the abundant water in these scenic hills comes a diversity of flora and fauna and almost half of Botswana's 250 butterfly species can be found here. **Butterflies** are particularly plentiful near Moeng College, Botswana's first secondary school.

### THE DASSIE'S TAIL

Dassies can often be seen sunning themselves on rocks and boulders. Batswana folklore states that in the beginning when God decided to give all the animals tails, the dassie did not receive his and was very sad at having been left out. The other animals felt so sorry for him that they told him to wait out on the rocky hilltops so that when God came back he would see the dassie first and would give him a tail of his own. So next time you see a dassie sitting out on a ledge scanning the sky, remember who he might be waiting for.

## TOWNS OF EASTERN BOTSWANA

The main road that crosses eastern Botswana linking Gaborone and Francistown is a double-lane tarred road.

The **Tropic of Capricorn** crosses this road 152km (91 miles) north of Gaborone. At this point a dirt road turns off to the east to the now closed border post of Buffel's Drift on the Limpopo River. From here there is a four-wheel-drive track north along the riverbank to the southern end of the Tuli Block farms. There is a gate to the private farm-lands, but traffic is permitted to those staying at the private camps or lodges along the river in this area.

### Mahalapye *

The town of Mahalapye lies just within the tropics, 198km (119 miles) from Gaborone. It is a busy, dusty little metropolis with numerous shops, garages, takeaways and stores lining the road as it meanders between the riverbed and the rocky *kopjes* that hem in the town. In the early 1990s the town grew considerably with the establishment of the Botswana Railways Headquarters here.

### Shoshong *

Just 30km (18 miles) west of Mahalapye is the historical village of Shoshong, once the old Ngwato capital from where Chief Khama gave permission to the ill-fated 'Thirstland Trekkers' to cross his territory in the late 1870s. It was here that **John Mackenzie** established a mission station where he lived for 14 years, during which time he played a crucial role in helping the chiefs secure British protection and halt the feared Boer expansion. The remains of his church can still be seen here, as well as the large flat 'church bell' stone which, when struck by another rock, resonated like a bell to hail the people to church.

### RESPECT THE PRESIDENT

Remember when entering official offices throughout Botswana that the President's photograph will be displayed. It is a sign of respect to remove any hat or headgear that you might be wearing in the presence of the President's photograph.

▶ *Opposite: The shepherd's tree is an important source of nutrition.*

▼ *Below: Safety is vital at the BCL copper and nickle mine in Selebi-Phikwe.*

## Palapye *

About 70km (42 miles) beyond Mahalapye is the crossroads to Serowe (see page 82) and Palapye where considerable coal deposits have been discovered. The main town of Palapye is a short distance east of the main road. Petrol is available here. Palapye is considered to be the powerhouse of Botswana; it is home to the Morupule power station, which supplies most of the country's needs. The original names of Mahalapye and Palapye are very similar, being Mhalatswe and Phalatswe respectively. Both refer to the impala antelope (Aepyceros melampus) which used to thrive in the area.

## Selebi-Phikwe *

Beyond Palapye the main road passes through stands of mopane woodland before reaching the eastern turn-off to the mining town of Selebi-Phikwe 88km (53 miles) southwest of Francistown. Many visitors to Botswana in the past have missed this town, located just over 50km (33 miles) off the main road, but it has grown into the third-largest urban centre in Botswana. With the completion of the tarred road from the Martin's Drift border post, Selebi-Phikwe is now a convenient halfway stopover between Johannesburg (via Ellisras) and Botswana's northern tourist attractions.

Originally there were two tiny places called Selebi and Phikwe, which straddled a large undiscovered deposit of copper and nickel in the area. When the mineral wealth of the area was discovered in the 1960s a mine and township was built in the woodland between the places with the combined name of Selebi-Phikwe.

The mining operations at Selebi-Phikwe have not been as successful as expected and the economy of the area has diversified into areas such as manufacturing and commerce. A power grid terminal was opened here in 1996 to carry electricity from South Africa through to Zimbabwe – the first stage of the Southern African Power Pool.

### THE SMELLY SHEPHERD'S TREE

The shepherd's tree (Boscia albitrunca) occurs throughout Botswana and is known as the 'tree of life', being an immensely important source of nutrition for both animals and humans. Its leaves have a high vitamin A content, the hollow trunks form natural reservoirs and the roots can be eaten raw or cooked, or can be roasted and ground into a satisfying coffee substitute. The roots also have preservative properties. The shepherd's tree flowers in spring after the first rains, with a profusion of small sweet-smelling yellow flowers. But be warned there is a subspecies called the smelly shepherd's tree (Boscia foetida) which is common in the Tuli area and, for all its virtues, when in flower it smells worse than a public toilet.

## BEST TIMES TO VISIT

**Game viewing** in this corner of Botswana is best from **April** to **December** when the animals congregate around the permanent water points. While the summer months from October to April can be extremely hot, and even during the winter, the day temperature can often reach as high as 35°C (95°F) while the nights are very cold.

## GETTING THERE

There is a regional airport at **Selebi-Phikwe** which is serviced by charter flights, but to reach the tourist areas of the Tuli Block one must fly into the Limpopo Valley Airfield from where you will need to be collected. There are no scheduled Air Botswana flights into Tuli, but there are regular charter flights which can be organized from any major centre in or outside Botswana. Flying time is about one and a half hours from Gaborone, Johannesburg or Harare. Customs and Immigration facilities are available at this landing strip for tourists flying into the area from outside Botswana.

**By road** there are several two-wheel- and four-wheel-drive routes. From Gauteng, drive to the Pont Drift border post via Ellisras and Alldays. From Zimbabwe, visitors can either cross into Botswana at Plumtree and go via Francistown, or go through Beit Bridge and approach Pont Drift via Musina. From Gaborone one can drive via Mahalapye and cross the Parr's Halt border post, though it is also possible to go via Palapye, or to turn right (east) at the Tropic of Capricorn and drive to Buffel's Drift on the Limpopo where you turn left (north) and enter the bottom end of the Tuli Block (four-wheel-drive is recommended for this route). From Francistown one can reach the Tuli Block either via Selebi-Phikwe or Palapye. Note that the Buffel's Drift border post has been closed for years and the other border posts across the Limpopo River are only open from 08:00–16:00.

## GETTING AROUND

As most of the Tuli area is private property travellers who are not booked into any of the lodges or camps cannot conduct their own game drives, save for sticking to the main road through the area and hoping for the best. But almost all of the private reserves offer their guests excellent guided day and night game drives as well as guided walks.

## WHERE TO STAY

As the contact numbers of the following establishments are subject to change, if you are having trouble contacting either their local or South African booking offices (with the prefix +27 numbers), try any of the established travel agents such as:

**Concorde Travel**, tel: 390 8142, fax: 316 4859.
**Harvey World Travel**, tel: 390 4360, fax: 390 5840.
**Skylink Travel**, tel: 316 2599, fax: 316 3023.
**Sunrise Travel & Tours**, tel: 318 7807, fax: 318 1925.
**TRL Travel**, tel: 390 0880, fax: 390 0836.
**Travel Star**, tel: 393 0065, fax: 393 1052.
**Travelwise**, tel: 390 3244, fax: 390 3245.

*Tuli*
LUXURY
**Mashatu Game Reserve**, tel: 264 5321 or 264 5263, e-mail: mashatu@malamala. com Selection of superb accommodation options in the largest private game reserve in southern Africa. Includes adventure and children's programmes.
**Nitani Lodge**, tel: +27 31 764 2346, e-mail: reservations@ nitani.co.za Five-star luxury on the banks of the Majali River focusing on archeology, ornithology and cultural heritage, plus the wildlife and gourmet cuisine.
**Tuli Safari Lodge**, tel: 264 5303, e-mail: info@tulilodge. com Luxury accommodation at the lodge and Molema Bush Camp. Excellent drives and guided walks.
**Kwa Tuli Island Camp**, tel: 7211 3688, e-mail: bookings @wildattuli.com Tented luxury safari camp with bar and restaurant in stunning location on an island in the Limpopo.

*MID-RANGE AND BUDGET*

**Limpopo River Lodge**, tel: 7210 6098, e-mail: elize@montaguhomes.co.za Comfortable self-catering lodge in the southern Tuli area, with chalets, rondavels and pool, situated right on the river's edge.

**Oasis Lodge**, tel: 7131 3399, e-mail: limlodge4@telkomsa. net Air-conditioned, *en-suite* rooms set in lush green lawns, with pool and restaurant, game drives and helicopter rides.

**Serolo Safari Camp**, tel: 7219 4495, e-mail: info@tulitrails. com Located on the flood plain of the Limpopo River, Serolo offers full-board or self-catering accommodation, and incredible trails and walking safaris.

**Shalimpo Island Camp**, tel: +27 21 686 6056, e-mail: coet@iafrica.com This small exclusive camp is set on a rocky kopje on an island overlooking the confluence of the Limpopo and Shashe rivers.

**Stevensford Game Reserve**, tel: 7138 1113, e-mail: reservations@stevensford gamereserve.com This private game farm offers self-catering lodges and camping. Activities include game drives, boat cruises, horse-riding, fishing and mountain biking.

*Mahalapye*
*BUDGET*

**Maeto Lodge**, tel: 472 0035, e-mail: maetolodge@yahoo.

com Centrally located two-star accommodation.

**Seduda Lodge**, tel: 473 0100/2, fax: 473 0101. Comfortable lodge in garden setting on Francistown road.

**Gaetsho Lodge**, tel: 472 0651. Centrally located affordable lodge with restaurant and bar.

**Oasis Lodge**, tel: 471 2081. Part of the Oasis chain.

*Palapye*
*MID-RANGE*

**Cresta Botsalo Hotel**, tel: 492 0245, e-mail: resbotsalo@ cresta.co.bw Comfortable facilities with good restaurant and swimming pool, situated right on the main road.

**Majestic Five Hotel**, tel: 492 1222. New four-star hotel with restaurant, bars and massive pool.

*BUDGET*

**Horizon Holiday Lodges,** tel: 492 4390/1.

**Palapye Hotel**, tel: 492 0277. With restaurant and bar.

*Selebi-Phikwe*
*MID-RANGE*

**Cresta Bosele Hotel**, tel: 261 0675, e-mail: resbosele@cresta. co.bw Centrally located hotel with excellent restaur-

ant in one of Botswana's fastest growing towns.

**Phokoje Bush Lodge**, tel: 260 1596. Three-star lodge and restaurant.

*BUDGET*

**Syringa Lodge & Spur**, tel: 261 0444, e-mail: syringa@syringa. co.bw On airport road, with popular Spur family restaurant as well as car-hire facilities.

## WHERE TO EAT

The lodges and camps in the Tuli Block are not open to casual visitors, but there are restaurants at all the hotels in the main centres in eastern Botswana as well as cafés and takeaways.

## TOURS AND EXCURSIONS

Generally independent tour operators do not organize excursions into the Tuli area, but all travel agents can arrange all-inclusive or self-catering trips to any of the lodges or camps in the area, tailored to match any particular budget.

## USEFUL CONTACTS

**Kalahari Air Services** for charters into the Tuli area; tel: 395 1804, e-mail: kasac@info.bw

| BOBONONG | J | F | M | A | M | J | J | A | S | O | N | D |
|---|---|---|---|---|---|---|---|---|---|---|---|---|
| MIN AVE TEMP. °C | 20 | 19 | 17 | 14 | 8 | 5 | 4 | 8 | 12 | 16 | 18 | 19 |
| MIN AVE TEMP. °F | 68 | 66 | 63 | 57 | 46 | 41 | 39 | 46 | 54 | 61 | 64 | 66 |
| MAX AVE TEMP. °C | 32 | 31 | 30 | 27 | 25 | 22 | 22 | 25 | 29 | 30 | 31 | 31 |
| MAX AVE TEMP. °F | 90 | 88 | 86 | 81 | 77 | 72 | 72 | 77 | 84 | 86 | 88 | 88 |
| RAINFALL mm | 71 | 80 | 32 | 28 | 4 | 3 | 0 | 0 | 4 | 25 | 38 | 63 |
| RAINFALL in | 2.8 | 3.2 | 1.3 | 1.1 | 0.2 | 0.1 | 0 | 0 | 0.2 | 1 | 1.9 | 2.5 |

# 6
# The Central Kalahari

In the middle of Botswana lies the heart of the Kalahari – a flat sea of sand in a dry and featureless world. But within this monotony a wealth of wildlife and breathtaking landscapes awaits discovery.

The shimmering façade of baked sand hides an incredible diversity of strangely adapted plant and animal life. There is the Devil's claw, a spiky weed pod that contains natural aspirin; the majestic gemsbok with a built-in air conditioner; and the distasteful dung beetle upon whom almost everyone's survival depends.

This expansive landscape has always held a magnetic attraction for man, and since the middle of the 19th century explorers have been drawn here, searching for undiscovered wealth. So far treasure and lost cities have eluded all, and many people have died trying to cross the dry interior. A rusty trail of broken, sun-bleached wagons can still be found littering the lost Missionaries' Road which once carved its way across this inhospitable interior, bringing with it the first early explorers.

### THE CENTRAL KALAHARI GAME RESERVE ***

Established in 1961 this massive reserve covers some 52,800km² (20,000 sq miles), just slightly smaller than the combined size of Holland and Belgium.

But, unlike other reserves which are usually set aside to protect animals, this area was originally intended as a sanctuary for its human inhabitants – it was the last domain of the nomadic San. Until recently there were still a few small groups of these remarkable

### DON'T MISS

*** **Cheetah** at the kill.
** The **vast openness** of wide game-filled plains.
* The **lion's roar** echoing against the black star-studded night sky.
* Following in the Owens' footsteps across the dry **Deception Pan**.

◄Opposite: The setting sun casts a crimson glow over the Kalahari landscape.

# THE CENTRAL KALAHARI

### CLIMATE

The short spring and autumn seasons from September to October and from April to May respectively are the best times to visit when it is neither too hot nor too cold. The temperatures can become unbearable in the summer months from November to March with day temperatures often exceeding 40°C (104°F), broken by occasional and violent thunderstorms. In winter the nights are bitterly cold with temperatures having been known to drop as low as -10°C (14°F)!

Stone Age people wandering through the wastes of the southern reserve, completely unaware of the encroaching 'civilized' world. The last of these San, or Bushmen as they were known, now reside in small village communities in the reserve at places like Xade, Xaka, Molapo and Metseamonong.

The Central Kalahari Game Reserve (CKGR) is remarkable for not just its vast open expanse and captivating 'big skies' but also for its **wildlife**. Game viewing is best in the northern half of the park in the hot months between December and April when the herds congregate around the water holes, but throughout the year you can expect to see most of the antelope and their accompanying predators, the lions, leopard, cheetah and hyena.

There are designated **camping sites** at Piper, Sunday and Leopard Pans as well as in the Passarge Valley where the Tau (meaning 'Lion') camp site is located. There are also camping sites in Deception Valley. When camping here, you need to bring all your own water and firewood.

### Deception Valley ★★★

Deception Valley is all that remains of a sprawling river bed that has long since dried up. Stretching across about 80km (48 miles) of the park's north, the valley is now covered with short grass, dotted with the occasional island of bushy trees. Some of the roots of the larger trees extend as far as 50m (165ft) below the surface to the water table, enabling them to survive the dry winters.

## WARNING: DEADLY GRASS

There are very real dangers awaiting the unwary traveller in the Kalahari. With the abundance of dry grass the conditions are unique and complacency could lead to tragedy in an area where the next passing vehicle could be many days or even months away.

- **Burning seeds:** With the low volumes of traffic the grass in the middle of the tracks can grow very tall and after rain it is heavy with long, black grass seeds. These can accumulate in crevices under the vehicle, packing into a solid mass particularly around the exposed exhaust area. Within minutes this flammable matrix can start to smoulder. When the car slows down or stops the woody material is engulfed in flames. If the area is grassy with telltale dark tasselled seeds, check under the vehicle every five minutes or so, clearing them away every time. It's also worth tying an old sack onto the engine grill to drag under the vehicle; this helps to disperse the seeds. If you are faced with a fire save your water, as that will be vital for surviving the following days waiting for help to arrive. Use a fire extinguisher if you have one, if not, try to smother the flames with the sand under the car and pinch any ruptured fuel lines to stop the fire from spreading.
- **Radiator damage:** Thousands of seeds can clog up radiator vents reducing efficiency and causing overheating. To protect against this, cover the radiator with a fine wire mesh to catch the seeds, and clear the mesh regularly. If the radiator does get clogged up the only thing to do is to clear it, and this often involves laborious hours of picking individual seeds out with a needle.
- **Burning grass:** There is a danger of a hot exhaust igniting grass under the vehicle. To avoid this do not pull off the road or stop in tall grass for any reason. If you want to stop, stop in the middle of the road where no grass will be in contact with the exhaust system. (In any case, driving off the road is prohibited in the national parks and permanently scars the fragile vegetation.)

The low canopies of these tree grove islands, usually made up of **umbrella thorn** (*Acacia tortilis*) and **buffalo thorn** (*Ziziphus mucronata*) provide shelter for game during the heat of the day and one can often see lion dozing in the shade of these thickets.

### Routes into the Central Kalahari Game Reserve

There are several routes into the reserve; the most well used is Matswere Gate via **Rakops. From Gaborone** drive from Palapye to Serowe, on to Letlhakane and the closed diamond-mining town of Orapa to Rakops which is 355km (215 miles) from Serowe. At the western edge of Rakops is a road signposted to the Central Kalahari Game Reserve, and 55km (33 miles) down this road is the park entrance.

For those looking for a real 4x4 challenge, a route can be taken via Khutse (*see* page 83). Exit Khutse's northern boundary into the Central Kalahari Game Reserve (CKGR) and drive to the San villages of Bape and Kumuchuru in the middle of the park, then head north via Molapo.

▼ *Below: The golden perennial grasses of the Kalahari stabilize the ancient fossil dunes.*

From Francistown take the Orapa road, skirting the southern side of the Mine Concession to join up with the Mopipi road and on to Rakops.

The road **from Maun** to the Central Kalahari Game Reserve (CKGR) has been upgraded, making the journey a lot quicker and easier. You can take the dirt turn-off to Makalamabedi and link through to Motopi and work your way down the cordon fence. The recommended route, however, is to go about 105km (63 miles) from Maun and just before the San pits turn south to the village of Matima where you join the new road that skirts the Makgadikgadi and Nxai Pan National Park down to Rakops.

The route **from Ghanzi** is definitely one for the adventurous. The turn-off is signposted 36km (22 miles) south of Ghanzi on the main Kang road to the San village of Xade which is 160km (100 miles) away. From Xade, where you must check in at the Wildlife Camp, take the northern track to Piper Pan which is 79km (48 miles) to the north. From Pipers, Deception Pan is another 80km (48 miles) northeast.

As most visitors to the CKGR drive in via Serowe it is worth exploring this scenic and historic village.

### SEROWE

Set in rocky hills 47km (28 miles) west of Palapye, Serowe is the capital of the Bangwato tribe, the largest of Botswana's Tswana tribes. With a population of over 70,000 people, this attractively located settlement is reputed to be the largest traditional tribal village in Africa. It is also the birthplace of the country's first president, Sir Seretse Khama, who is buried with his wife, Lady Ruth, and other important members of the Royal House, including King Khama III, at the summit of **Thathaganyane Hill**. It is worth visiting the cemetery to appreciate the wonderful view.

## DIAMONDS

Botswana is one of the world's largest diamond producers and has three very rich, massive open-cast mines, all situated in the Kalahari. **Orapa**, near the Central Kalahari National Park, was the first to be discovered in 1967, followed several years later by smaller **Letlhakane**. Although Letlhakane bears less carats in terms of volume it has one of the highest percentages of gem-quality stones in the world. Then in the early 1980s **Jwaneng** was opened in the southern Kalahari; its pit is now twice the size of the famous Big Hole in Kimberley. An undeveloped diamond pipe has been discovered at Gope in the CKGR, and a smaller mine is being planned in the Tuli Block area, to start production once the world diamond market fully recovers.

### Khama III Memorial Museum *

At the base of the hill is the Khama III Memorial Museum which occupies the 'Red House' built especially for this celebrated chief in 1910. The museum, in addition to natural history displays, commemorates the Ngwato and San culture and history.

Serowe was also home to the well-known South African novelist **Bessie Head** who wrote numerous books including *Serowe: Village of the Rain Wind* based on local village life. Many of her letters and manuscripts are preserved in the museum.

There are several petrol stations and a choice of shops and supermarkets, making Serowe a convenient supply stop for travellers venturing into the Central Kalahari.

### The Khama Rhino Sanctuary ***

In 1992 the Khama Rhino Sanctuary was established on 4300ha (10,625 acres) donated by the Ngwato Land Board in response to a proposal by the people of Serowe for a game reserve to be set up around Serowe Pan to protect the last of the nation's endangered rhino. The sanctuary, whose patron is the Bangwato Paramount Chief and President of Botwana, Ian Khama, is 25km (15 miles) northeast of the town on the Orapa road.

Home to 34 rhino, the Khama Rhino Sanctuary is also shared with giraffe, zebra, wildebeest, hartebeest, leopard, hyena and more than 230 bird species. The reserve has a good network of game-viewing roads and well serviced camp sites and chalets, including a very comfortable double-storey 'A' frame. There is also a good restaurant that specializes in tasty traditional dishes. Rhino and giraffe tracking and nature walks can be arranged as well as guided game drives and very good night drives.

### KHUTSE GAME RESERVE ***

Although large by normal standards, Khutse Game Reserve, covering 2590km² (985 sq miles), is dwarfed by

◄ *Opposite: Traditional crafts are displayed in the Khama 'Red House' Museum in Serowe.*
▼ *Below: Translocated rhino settle into their well-guarded new home at the Khama Rhino Sanctuary.*

# THE CENTRAL KALAHARI

## THE DEVIL'S CLAW

The **wild grapple** (*Harpagophytum procumbens*), which grows in the remote Kalahari sands is locally know as Devil's claw due to its hard spiny pods which hook and stab into almost anything. These plants are one of Botswana's most effective traditional medicines. The plant contains **natural aspirin** and, while it has been used in Africa for centuries, modern scientists are only now recognizing it as being as effective as synthetic drugs in the treatment of a range of ailments including rheumatism, hypertension, gastrointestinal and skin problems, diabetes, neuralgia and arteriosclerosis. Tests have proven that grapple healed at least 60% of arthritis cases. While in Botswana be sure to try Devil's claw and your holiday could result in improved health.

its vast neighbour, the Central Kalahari Game Reserve, with whom it shares its northern boundary. Being close to Gaborone it is a popular weekend destination, where visitors can appreciate the true peace and quiet of the Kalahari – and get a chance to see the majestic black-maned Kalahari lions.

The name 'Khutse' means 'the place where you can kneel down to drink', so it is hardly surprising that there are more than 60 seasonal pans dotting the park's flat, grassy landscape. But this flatness is ideal country for cheetah, who love the openness to reach their phenomenal speeds of up to 120kph (75mph) to run down their prey.

### Camp Sites

There is an established camp site with ablution blocks and running water at the entrance gate where park entry fees have to be paid. At the other 20 camp sites within the reserve there are, at most, only pit latrines and certainly no running water, so be sure to fill up at this main camp. The water here is unfortunately rather brackish. **Khutse Camp Site** is 13km (8 miles) from the entrance gate and is situated between a couple of open pans at the junction of the large loop road around the park.

### The Pans

**Golalabodimo Pan** is right at the park gate. Almost directly after this pan is a turn-off to the north. This goes to the distant village of Gope in the Central Kalahari Game Reserve and should not be taken.

Going northwest the road passes **Motailane Pan** which has a water hole. This is followed by **Tshilwane Pan** bordering the Central Kalahari Game Reserve. The third pan, popular for its game concentrations, is **Mahurushele Pan** and there are a couple of camp sites near its edge. Close by is a camp site under a shady camel thorn tree near **Sekushuwe Pan**, while 11km (7 miles) further north at **Khankhe Pan** is a very attractive camp site on the sand dune overlooking the pan.

Central Kalahari Game Reserve

Khankhe Pan

Sekushuwe Pan

Mahurushele Pan

Game Scout Camp

Tshilwane Pan

Motailane Pan

Molose Pan

Khutse Pan

Golalabodimo Pan

Khutse Game Reserve

Moreswe Pan

Mabuakolobe Pan

◄ Left: The magnificent leopard which, weight for weight, is the strongest of the world's cats.

◄◄ Opposite: A grassy pan, damp from a local borehole, is one of the few sources of permanent water for the wildlife in Khutse.

Khankhe Pan is actually within the Central Kalahari Game Reserve so do not drive further north from Khankhe Pan; the track heads off a great distance into the arid semidesert and should you get lost or break down help will be a long way away. Take the loop road that heads back in a southerly direction through open grassland for almost 30km (18 miles) before reaching the three camp sites at **Molose water hole**.

**Note:** camping is not permitted near this water hole as it disturbs the animals' access to the water.

**Molose Pan** has a distinctive sand dune overlooking its western edge and is the most reliable supply of drinking water in the reserve so considerable concentrations of game are often to be found here.

Further to the south is **Moreswe Pan**, with more camp sites equipped with pit latrines. This is probably the most popular camping area in the whole park with its reputation for concentrations of game and tall, attractive trees.

There is another water hole here, but its water is extremely saline and undrinkable except when it is diluted by rain water. Even so, many animals visit this borehole for the salt and minerals that they derive from both the water and the pan surface. In fact, the holes in the pan surface near the reservoir have been dug by gemsbok who, along with various animals, actually eat the mineral-rich soil. Be sure to look out for cheetah which are often sighted around Moreswe Pan.

## THE LAST GREAT PLAIN

Unfortunately the delicate ecosystem of the Central Kalahari is at risk and soon will change or even disappear altogether. Since the 1980s animal populations have fallen dramatically with wildebeest and hartebeest numbers now less than 15% of what they were just a few decades ago. Hopefully, through the realization of its money-earning potential and the lobbying of the environmentally conscious international community, this last vestige of wild Africa will be protected for future generations.

## PANS OF THE PAST

The pans in Khutse are relics of the superlake that once covered northern Botswana. The geology of this area began to take shape after the glaciation of Antarctica five million years ago, when southern Africa became drier. Easterly winds built up long sand dunes across the sub-continent which, when wetter times returned, channelled water into the superlake. The Meratswe River Valley which passes through Khutse was one of these channels which linked up with Lake Xau and on to the Makgadikgadi. It is believed that this river carried a great deal of water north-wards about 15,000 years ago, but with tectonic warping of this lower end of the Great East African Rift Valley the flow of water was stopped and it dried up leaving the pans dotted across Khutse's shallow valley floor.

Remember that it is **forbidden** to drive across any of the pans and, if you do – even if you follow existing tracks across these fragile features – you will be asked to leave the park, as this causes irreparable damage. While you can walk across the pans, the Department of Wildlife and National Parks cannot be held responsible for your safety!

### Routes into Khutse Game Reserve

The only practical route to Khutse Game Reserve is from Gaborone via Molepolole. Molepolole, which is 50km (30 miles) north of the Capital, is the last major village on the way to Khutse. From here take the tar road a further 65km (40 miles) to Letlhakeng. There is a small petrol station at Letlhakeng, but the tar ends here and from here on four-wheel-drive is very necessary.

Although Letlhakeng marks the start of the dry Kalahari sands, not so long ago this area was reputed to be lush. Several strong freshwater springs attracted large numbers of rhino, elephant and buffalo and, as a legacy of this now long-forgotten past, the name Letlhakeng means 'place of reeds'. From here it is a further 120km (72 miles) to the Khutse Game Scout Camp on a poorly signposted road via the tiny villages of Khudumelapye and Salajwe, after which the road becomes very sandy and difficult to negotiate.

The sand road is often crisscrossed by secondary tracks, some leading off to cattleposts and others just routes around sandy patches. Always stick to the most well-used track as it is likely to be the right one and keep following the green National Park signs. The 210km (130-mile) journey will take about four hours.

Almost at the entrance to Khutse Game Reserve is a small San settlement where crafts can be bought. Be considerate of these people's privacy and do not wander uninvited into their camp or take photographs without having at least asked permission.

▼ *Below: The rolling grass-lands of the Central Kalahari stretch far beyond the horizon.*

## BEST TIMES TO VISIT

The spring months of **September** and **October** and the autumn months of **April** and **May** are the most comfortable months to visit when it is neither too hot nor too cold. **Game viewing** is excellent in Khutse from **July** to **September** when large herds congregate around the pans. Deception Valley in the Central Kalahari Game Reserve is usually comfortable all year round. While generally good, the **game viewing** in the Central Kalahari is best after the **first rains** (**December/January**) when the landscape is transformed into a lush green parkland. Khutse can get crowded over long weekends, particularly Easter when people from Gaborone tend to visit.

## GETTING THERE

It is not practical to fly into the Central Kalahari as you need to have vehicles on the ground. The best route into CKGR is therefore via **Rakops** from Gaborone or Francistown and from Matima if you are coming from Maun. Khutse is best approached via Molepolole.

## GETTING AROUND

The choice is to hire a car, join a package tour or to use your own 4x4 vehicle. Car hire can be arranged through either **Avis**, tel: 395 3745, fax: 391 2461, e-mail : botswanares@avis.co.za **Budget**, tel: 390 2030, fax: 390 2028, e-mail: Botswana@budget.co.za

**Select Car Rental**, tel: 397 1240, fax: 390 1141. **Limit Car Rental**, tel: 393 2825, e-mail: limitcar@ botsnet.bw

## WHERE TO STAY

There are no lodges or hotels in the national parks and camping is only allowed at designated camp sites. But there are luxury lodges adjacent to the parks:

### Central Kalahari Game Reserve
**Dinaka Safari Lodge**, tel: 680 0251, e-mail: info@dinaka.com All-inclusive tented camp on a 20,000ha (49,500-acre) game ranch on the northern edge of CKGR. **Haina Kalahari Lodge**, tel: 683 0238/9, email: reservations@ hainakalaharilodge.com Luxury safari tents and thatched lodge and boma. Bushman culture, quad-biking and game viewing. **Kalahari Plains Camp**, tel: 686 0086. Perfectly appointed Wilderness Safaris camp just 20km (12 miles) from Deception Valley.

### Khutse
**Khutse Kalahari Lodge**, tel: 318 7163,

e-mail: reservations@ khutsekalaharilodge.com Luxury lodge at the eastern gate of Khutse. Offering game viewing and the unique 'Bushman Walk'.

## WHERE TO EAT

Apart from a few traditional restaurants and takeaways in Serowe and Letlhakane (such as Grandma's Kitchen, Masa and Northgate) there are no other places to eat in the Central Kalahari and visitors must be completely self-sufficient.

## TOURS AND EXCURSIONS

There are no regular excursions into the Central Kalahari, but tailored trips can be organized through any reputable travel agent in Botswana.

## WHAT TO TAKE

In the Central Kalahari water and fuel are vital as there are no supplies anywhere. From the middle of the reserve the nearest town of any size is over 300km (185 miles) away in any direction! Take at least 5 litres (9 pints) of water per person per day, plus an extra 20%. Due to the fragile environment also bring in all your own firewood, including kindling.

| KALAHARI | J | F | M | A | M | J | J | A | S | O | N | D |
|---|---|---|---|---|---|---|---|---|---|---|---|---|
| MIN AVE TEMP. °C | 19 | 19 | 17 | 13 | 8 | 5 | 5 | 7 | 12 | 16 | 18 | 19 |
| MIN AVE TEMP. °F | 66 | 66 | 63 | 55 | 46 | 41 | 41 | 45 | 54 | 61 | 64 | 66 |
| MAX AVE TEMP. °C | 33 | 32 | 31 | 39 | 27 | 24 | 24 | 27 | 31 | 33 | 33 | 33 |
| MAX AVE TEMP. °F | 91 | 90 | 88 | 84 | 81 | 75 | 75 | 81 | 88 | 91 | 91 | 91 |
| RAINFALL mm | 102 | 77 | 57 | 33 | 7 | 1 | 0 | 1 | 5 | 22 | 47 | 72 |
| RAINFALL in | 4 | 3 | 2.2 | 1.3 | 0.3 | 0 | 0 | 0 | 0.2 | 0.9 | 1.9 | 2.8 |

# 7
# Chobe National Park

Established in 1967 and covering 10,600km² (4030 sq miles), this vast northern park, which is named after the Chobe River, is the second largest national park in Botswana and is home to the greatest concentration of game on the southern African subcontinent.

This park, and much of northern Botswana, is set to become the main attraction of the new **Kavango Zambezi Transfrontier Conservation Area** (KAZA TFCA). This ambitious scheme is planned to become the world's biggest conservation area. It is envisaged to span approximately 444,000km² (172,000 sq miles), taking in 36 national parks and game reserves across the five countries of Botswana, Angola, Namibia, Zambia and Zimbabwe. In 2011 the presidents of these five countries signed a treaty which formally established the Kavango Zambezi TFCA, moving it from dream to reality.

Like the KAZA TFCA, **Chobe National Park** encompasses a diverse range of habitats, from the dense riverine forests and swamplands of Chobe and Linyanti to the mopane forests of Nogatsaa, and then across to the open grassy plains and rocky kopje outcrops of Savuti in the southwest.

Chobe is the site of a dramatic zebra migration. At this time the roads become almost impassable, congested with tens of thousands of animals forming a solid mass moving across the landscape. Throughout the year herds of elephant and buffalo can also be seen drinking along the river's edge, their numbers swelling into the hundreds and sometimes thousands during the dry season.

## DON'T MISS

*** Watching the sunset from a **river barge**.
** Catching the fighting **tigerfish** in the Chobe.
** Finding **cheetah** at the kill in Savuti's grasslands.
** Being surrounded by thousands of **migrating zebra**.
** Spotting the rare **Chobe bushbuck** in riverine forest.
** Drifting past hippo grazing on **Sedudu Island**.
* A day trip to the awesome **Victoria Falls**.

◄ *Opposite: The wide, slow-moving Chobe River defines the edge of the national park.*

# CHOBE NATIONAL PARK

## CLIMATE

The Chobe National Park can become uncomfortably hot from November to March, and the rain (heaviest from December to February) can make the central and south-ern roads impassable. There is little to no rain in winter (April to October) and while the day temperatures seldom drop below 25°C (77°F), the nights and early morning can be bitterly cold, particularly between May and August.

## KASANE **

This scenic little town just east of the park entrance gate is the main point of entry into Chobe National Park, and is just 12km (7 miles) west of Kazungula at the end of the main highway.

The boundary of the Chobe National Park butts right up to the western edge of the town and, as it is unfenced, many animals including elephant and hippo can be seen wandering casually through the streets and camp sites of Kasane.

There are numerous shops, garages, banks, hotels and lodges in the town, which is serviced by a major international airport located just 4km (2.5 miles) from the town centre.

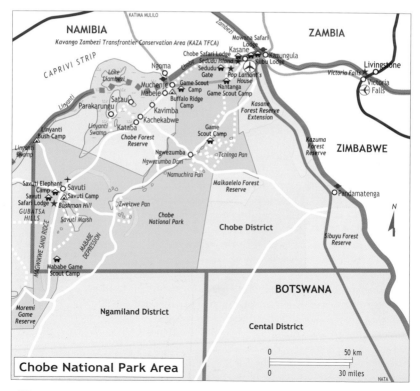

Chobe National Park Area

The crumpled remains of an ancient and once huge baobab tree (*Adansonia digitata*) can be seen from the main road in the police station grounds. The trunk is hollow and the tree was used as the local jail for many years before the current brick structure behind it was built.

## Kasane Rapids and Hot Springs ★★

A short distance out of Kasane in the game corridor between Kasane and Kazungula, you will find the Kasane Rapids just east of Mowana Safari Lodge. The lodge is build round an 800-year-old baobab *(mowana)* tree and overlooks the river near the start of the rapids.

Slightly further downstream the river flows over a pronounced seam of basalt rock, speeding it on its way towards the awaiting Zambezi. There are several picnic sites in this area and it is well worth a visit, particularly as a wealth of riverine birds can be seen including several unusual species such as the African finfoot and halfcollared kingfisher.

Several kilometres further along the main road are the Kasane Hot Springs. While it is a rustic facility, the local tribesmen believe that these warm, brackish springs hold soothing medicinal properties.

## Sedudu Island ★★★

The large flat grassy expanse of Sedudu Island fills the central channel of the Chobe River opposite Kasane. This island has always been contested between Namibia and Botswana, and is reputed to have been the site of the first shots of World War I fired between the Germans and the British. The debate was eventually resolved in 2000 with Sedudu being confirmed as part of Botswana after an international court studied the riverbed to determine exactly where the boundary ran. This has been an important decision as it is now part of the national park and is a vital grazing site for countless buffalo and elephant.

### A FISHERMAN'S PARADISE

Having remained undiscovered for a long time, the Chobe River has become an extremely popular fishing destination with over 90 different species of fish to be found in the wide waterways off Kasane. Over 20 of these varieties are popular table or sport fish, such as bream and the fighting tigerfish, and fully organized fishing safaris or private boat and tackle hire can be easily arranged at any of the lodges in Kasane or Kazungula.

▼ Below: Mowana Safari Lodge dominates the Chobe river bank.

# CHOBE NATIONAL PARK

▲ Above: A field worker tends tomatoes in a commercial plot just outside Kasane.
▼ Below: The memorial stone to 'Pop' Lamont, Serondela's last resident.

The main route into the national park is located 2km (1.2 miles) west of Kasane. This entrance, which is called Sedudu Gate, is near the airport at the end of the main tar road through the village. From Sedudu gate the road also goes across to Ngoma gate some 59km (37 miles) to the west and onward to Savuti. Soon after this gate is a turn-off to the left through Sedudu Valley which joins the Ngoma road to the Nantanga Pans 20km (12 miles) away. There are several water holes along the Sedudu Valley road as well as many large dead trees; these died when the valley last flooded. This is ideal terrain for seeing the area's considerable leopard population.

## THE RIVER FRONTAGE

Along the 15km (9 miles) of river frontage between Kasane and the remains of Serondela the road branches into numerous loops, many of them following the river flood plain and offering some of the best game viewing to be found anywhere in Africa with huge resident herds of buffalo and attending lion. The road network is well-developed and maintained and the concentrations and variety of other game, especially in winter, are overwhelming. It is possible to negotiate most of these tracks in two-wheel-drive vehicles, but if you are in two-wheel-drive do not venture any further into the park which can only be done in four-wheel-drive. The Game Scouts at the main gate recommend that you stick to the main roads.

Shortly after the national park's gate is the turn-off to the luxury Chobe Chilwero Lodge followed within a few kilometres by the Chobe Game Lodge, made famous by Richard Burton and Elizabeth Taylor.

### Serondela ★★★

Serondela, 15km (9 miles) upstream from the main entrance to the national park, started its life in the 1930s as a veterinary camp and timber mill. Considering the denuded landscape in this area now, it is hard to imagine that just 80 years ago Serondela was covered with tall **teak forests** that supported a milling industry. Much of the marginal flood plain between Kasane and Serondela is now covered in dense green groves of **feverberry** (*Croton megalobotrys*) and woolly **caper bushes** (*Capparis tomentosa*), encroaching on the roads beneath the last remains of the tall and very dead white-wooded trunks of the former forest. The seeds of the feverberry tree are very effective in the treatment of malaria, hence its name, while the long arched branches of the woolly caper bushes provide perfect shelter for both lions and leopards, so don't consider leaving your vehicle.

Between Kasane and Serondela there are very high concentrations of game and one is almost guaranteed to see some of Chobe's 70,000 elephant – as well as buffalo and lions. The bird life is astounding and you are likely to see an array of unusual water birds including the amazing African skimmers (*Rynchops flavirostris*).

There used to be a national parks camp site at Serondela overlooking the river, but this has been moved to Ihaha where there are significantly upgraded facilities including

## THE ELEPHANT DEBATE

Chobe has the highest concentration of elephants in the world with a total population of more than 70,000 individuals, and they are all Kalahari elephants, the largest of all known elephant subspecies. Consequently there is massive pressure on the local natural resources to sustain such a large population of these leviathans, which is why there is such bitter debate about the validity of CITES and the ban on elephant hunting in southern Africa. Whatever the outcome of this argument the Chobe National Park is still the best place in the world to see the majestic African elephant.

▼ *Below: A herd of buffalo fills the Chobe flood plain.*

▲ *Above: The horns of the majestic sable antelope provide excellent protection against lions.*

## THE AFRICAN SKIMMER

The Chobe River is one of the best places to see the strange and colourful African skimmer (*Rynchops flavirostris*). This reasonably large, short-legged bird is distinctive for its unique bill structure, with the lower mandible being much bigger and longer than the upper one. To feed, it flies just above the surface skimming the water with its blade-like bottom jaw and scooping up little fish, which is why it is called a skimmer. These birds are mainly found from the Okavango to the mouth of the Zambezi, and breed from July to October on sandbanks along the river course. One favoured breeding site is the tiny 'Skimmer Island' just west of Sedudu Island, but do not approach too close as these birds may abandon their nests.

hot showers and flush toilets and a very attractively designed reception office.

At Ngoma Gate, near the Namibian border-post, there is a private camp site called **Buffalo Ridge Camp Site,** which has reasonable facilities and offers travellers an overnight option on the long journey between Kasane and Savuti. The beautiful **sable antelope** (*Hippotragus niger*) are often seen in this Ngoma Gate area, while in late winter they tend to spread out along much of the river frontage towards Serondela.

Over 440 bird species have been recorded along this riverine section of the park, including many water birds such as the **malachite kingfisher** and the strangely beaked **African skimmer**. Chobe is also famous for the huge colonies of bright **carmine bee-eaters** which nest in the vertical river banks and can be seen in their hundreds acrobatically hawking insects over the river throughout the summer months.

## NOGATSAA AND TCHINGA

This pan-speckled grassy woodland lies some 70km (42 miles) due south of Serondela near the eastern park boundary. After the rains the pans hold water for several months making this very remote and often overlooked area one of the finest game-viewing regions in the country.

The two old camp sites and the game scout camp at Nogatsaa and Tchinga have all been shut down and removed so visitors can not longer overnight in the area. But the countryside around Nogatsaa, **Namuchira** and **Tchinga Pans** offers a very rewarding game-viewing excursion on the trip between Ihaha and Savuti. The area attracts a large number and great diversity of **game**, including prides of well-fed lion. From August to October the elephant breeding herds concentrate near the pans, before they head back towards the river frontage near Serondela. Being quite open the area can be windy in August and September.

This part of the national park is also the best place to

see Africa's **largest antelope**, the eland (*Taurotragus oryx*), which stands almost 2m (7ft) tall. Other animals often seen here include sable, roan antelope, leopard and cheetah.

## Routes to Nogatsaa

There are two routes from Kasane. The first is the road through Sedudu Valley, which, although very sandy is usually very rewarding for elephant, lion and leopard sightings, not to mention the thousands of resident impala. The second route is from Nantanga and is just under 50km (30 miles), but take great care in the rainy season as the area around Nogatsaa is black cotton soil which, when wet, is virtually impassable.

## Ngwezumba Dam *

Ngwezumba Dam no longer holds much water, its wall having been washed away by the drought-breaking rains in 1988. However, it can still offer very rewarding game viewing of the wildlife found in the area. The road past Ngwezumba goes on to Savuti some 114km (69 miles) away via the complex of pans at Zweizwe.

## SAVUTI ★★★

This famous corner of the Chobe National Park has been hailed as Africa's prime wildlife area. The annual zebra migration passes through it; sightings of leopard, cheetah and wild dog are not uncommon; and it is here

◄ *Left: A cluster of elephants enjoy a late afternoon drink at the river.*

## RARE ANTELOPE

The Chobe National Park is the only place you are likely to see several very rare species of antelope. They include:

**Chobe bushbuck (Kobus ellipsiprymnus)** – Unique to this area these beautiful bushbuck are slightly redder than the more common Southern and East African species. These animals can be seen in the evenings under the woolly caper bushes between Kasane and Serondela.

**Puku (Kobus vardoni)** – Similar to impala, they are however slightly smaller and redder lacking the distinctive markings of the impala and lechwe with whom they often associate.

**Oribi (Ourebia ourebi)** – Similar to steenbok with a whiter belly. These rare animals are the world's smallest grazing antelope and can be seen grazing on new grass in recently burnt areas.

**Sharpe's grysbok (Raphicerus sharpei)** – Smaller and darker than steenbok these secretive, nocturnal animals can live close to human habitation and can be seen in the cultivated lands or plots in and around Kasane.

that you'll find the greatest concentration of that king of all beasts, *Panthera leo*.

The main attraction of Savuti is the abundance of game and predators to be seen; at any time of year the sizes of herds can be staggering, while sightings of lion and spotted hyena are almost guaranteed.

The Savuti area covers almost 5000km² (1900 sq miles) in the southwestern corner of the park, encompassing the Savuti Marsh, which is now a vast open plain, the Mababe Depression and the Magwikwe Sand Ridge.

The **camp site** at Savuti has been upgraded and offers very attractive views overlooking the currently dry Savuti River channel. But be aware that the lions and hyenas often visit this camp site at night.

### Savuti Marsh ★★★

This marsh is originally what attracted the vast numbers of game to Savuti, providing an unlimited supply of water and rich pastures in an otherwise arid landscape. The game settled permanently in the area as did their predators and the lion and hyena populations grew dramatically, sustained by limitless prey.

According to the reports of early explorers the Savuti Channel filling the marsh flowed regularly between 1850 and 1880. It then suddenly dried up for almost 80 years before flowing again in 1957. This flow continued until 1982 when it once again stopped, only to start again in 2010.

▶ *Right: Hippos wallow in a pool in the Savuti Channel.*

To explain this flow, which is quite unrelated to the volume of the Linyanti River, geologists have measured the drop along the course of the Savuti Channel which is just a tiny 1 in 5300 over its entire length. Experts now believe that in order to stop the water flow the ground level of the Mababe Depression must be raised by as much as 9m (30ft) by the continual heaving and buckling of the faults in the area. Northern

▲ *Above: Impala, Botswana's most common antelope.*

Botswana is at the tail end of the active Great East African Rift Valley which causes this ground buckling and which influences the river flows.

Whether the Savuti river channel is wet or dry when you visit, from the camp site you will see a very noticeable line of dead trees that stand like gaunt sun-bleached sentries along the length of the riverbed. These trees were flood victims, drowned when the river started flowing again in the 1950s, by which time the channel was completely overgrown.

With the final drying of the Savuti Marsh, it has changed from a perennial wetland to semidesert in just a few short decades. Even the natural water table has dropped without the replenishment of the marsh, and the route of vehicles is now marked for miles around by the billowing black dust that drifts behind them.

Fortunately there are many natural pans in Savuti which hold water into the winter months, after which the animals must rely on the three pumped water holes, which see ever-increasing concentrations of game as other supplies dry up. In the last months before the rains (September and October) visitors must contend with soaring temperatures, but boreholes provide some splendid game viewing with droves of elephants, kudu, impala, buffalo, wildebeest, sable,

### THE GROUND HORNBILL

The massive glossy black, red-faced ground hornbill (*Bucorvus leadbeateri*) which stands over 1m (3½ft) high is common to this area. These birds are called 'Lehututu' in Setswana after their deep booming call which, when heard, is reputed to be a sign of rain. While these birds are not sacred, they are still treated with care by the local people who believe that if you harm a ground hornbill, its mate will hound you to your death, cursing you with its endless lamenting call. Ground hornbill nests are very seldom seen, usually made in holes in trees high off the ground or in rocky cliff faces where they are unlikely to be disturbed.

lion, hyena, and the occasional cheetah vying for a chance to drink.

When the rains return the pans fill and lush green grass carpets the plains. With the rains come the zebra, moving in their thousands down from Linyanti into the area of the Savuti Marsh and the Mababe Depression.

## Mababe Depression *

The Mababe Depression is edged by the Magwikwe Sand Ridge which traces a semicircular line for 100km (60 miles) to the north and west of the Savuti Marsh. This ancient feature, measuring 20m (65ft) in height and over 175m (540ft) in width, provides a gruelling challenge to drivers trying to cross it.

## Gubatsa Hills **

The seven Gubatsa Hills, which rise almost 90m (280ft) above the flat landscape and overlook the mouth of the Savuti Channel, provide fascinating evidence of the once great Makgadikgadi superlake. The northeastern faces of these hills have been cleaved into almost vertical cliffs by the millennia of waves that have pounded them, while on their leeward side are piles of beach pebbles rounded by the water's action.

## San Paintings **

There are over 20 San painting sites to be found in the rocky hills in Savuti. Most are badly faded, but the best, which depict a variety of recognizable game including a puff adder and a hippo, can be seen on the eastern side of **Bushman Hill**. These artworks have been dated at over 3000 years old. While it is generally not permitted to get out of your vehicle in the national park, one can do so at Bushman Hill and a rough track leads the way to the paintings. There is a very large

▼ *Below: Thousands of zebra gather, ready to start their migration.*

◀ Left: In a field of golden grass the fingers of a dead tree trace across a Savuti sky.

baobab tree near Bushman Hill which is worth a visit.

The sandy soils of the Savuti support a variety of grasses, especially in the marsh area, which is dotted with tiny 'islands' of feverberry bushes and the larger raintrees (*Lonchocarpus capassa*). To the south in the Mababe Depression there is less vegetation with the area being predominantly covered with scrub thorn-bushes. However, throughout the sandy soils of Savuti wild sage bushes (*Pechuelloeschea leubnitziae*) grow well, giving the area a distinctive and pleasant smell.

### Routes to Savuti

Many travellers with the time to spare choose to drive **from Maun** through Moremi Game Reserve into Savuti out via Kasane, taking in the country's major tourist attractions. If you are considering this route, exit Moremi at North Gate by crossing the bridge over the River Khwai. The road continues eastwards across very sandy terrain until you enter the Chobe National Park. Turn left at the first fork in the road and continue north until you reach the Mababe Gate 56km (35 miles) south of Savuti, where all visitors must register. Ten kilometres (6 miles) beyond this office is another fork in the road. Both routes lead to the Savuti camp site. The road to the left is slightly longer and follows the sand ridge capped with its mantle of camel thorn and Kalahari apple-leaf trees, while the one to the right

### THE ZEBRA MIGRATION

Botswana is the site of two separate zebra migrations. One is between **Linyanti** and **Savuti** with zebra arriving in Savuti in late November. They foal in Savuti and return to Linyanti between February and April. With the drying of Savuti, the zebra may change their migratory pattern as ultimately there won't be enough water to sustain them. The other smaller and lesser known migration occurs in the **Makgadikgadi**, but tragically the numbers of zebra in this migration were decimated during the drought of the 1980s. Their numbers have never recovered.

## PEL'S FISHING OWL

The Linyanti swamp and the Okavango Delta are the best places to see the remarkable Pel's fishing owl (*Skotopelia peli*), although you are much more likely to hear their eerie wailing scream. These birds have a massive wingspan of over 1.5m (5ft), giving them the strength to lift fish weighing over 2kg (4.5lb) straight out of the water. Most owls have feathered legs, but Pel's fishing owls have long scaly claws and rough soles for gripping their slippery prey. Their eyesight is highly developed, even compared with other owls, and at night they perch 1 to 2m (3 to 6ft) above the water studying the depths for fish, which form the majority of their diet. They also eat frogs, crabs, mussels and young crocodiles.

goes via the marsh across treacherous black cotton soil, making both alternatives extremely challenging. In the wet season go left, in the dry season go right. The total distance from North Gate to Savuti is 110km (66 miles).

**From Kasane** one can drive either via Serondela and Ngoma Gate or via Nogatsaa and around the Savuti Marsh. The road via Serondela is approximately 170km (100 miles) and is direct, leading out of the park at Ngoma, past the villages of Kavimba and Kachikau on the edge of the Liambezi flood plain, though deep sand dunes can hamper your progress. The road then takes you back into the park cutting directly southwest to the camp site.

**From Nogatsaa** take the road to Ngwezumba Dam, and then follow the track along the river course for a full 120km (72 miles) before you reach Savuti, marked by Quarry Hill with its huge distinctive baobab tree nestling next to it.

## LINYANTI ★★★

In the furthest corner of the Chobe National Park lies the forgotten paradise of Linyanti. Secluded and uncrowded, this short strip of swampy river frontage is reminiscent of the Okavango's permanent waterways with papyrus-lined lagoons, reedbeds and a towering canopy of trees.

The Linyanti Swamp covers an area of almost 900km² (340 sq miles), which follows the river and fills the area between the converging courses of the Kwando and Linyanti rivers. The national park only touches the river for a short section on the far eastern edge of the swamp.

The wildlife is plentiful, especially in the dry winter months when great concentrations of elephant, buffalo, and zebra congregate along the river, with giraffe, impala and the unusual roan antelope being seen in the forests. The bird life is diverse, if not overwhelming in its numbers. Water birds, including pelican, are common while you are likely to hear, if not see, Pel's fishing owl.

The wilderness areas around the park have for many years been hunting concessions, making the game, even within the park boundaries, wary and shy of humans. However, many of the hunting safari operators now concentrate more on photographic safaris, which has improved the quality of game viewing in the area, especially with the vast herds of elephants that can be seen in the dry season.

### Linyanti Camp Site ★★★

The remote public camp site at Linyanti 39km (24 miles) northeast of Savuti is possibly the most attractive in Botswana, set in deep shade overlooking the papyrus and reedbeds that line the river, where resident hippo can be heard grunting to each other. There are well-maintained ablutions which include flush toilets and hot showers.

Outside the Chobe National Park along the river are several private camps which offer luxury tented accommodation and have their own private landing strips making access easier. Being outside the park, night drives and game walks can be arranged from these camps.

### Routes to Linyanti

One can drive to Linyanti from either Savuti or Kasane, but both roads traverse patches of deep sand.

**From Savuti** take the Kasane road until you see a signposted turning to Linyanti on the left just before the water hole and landing strip. After 8km (5 miles) there is a fork where you bear to the right and continue straight for approximately 30km (18 miles) until you reach Linyanti.

**From Kasane**, take the Savuti road via Ngoma Gate and Kavimba until you reach the Chobe National Park sign where the road re-enters the park. Turn right here and follow the straight firebreak cutline for about 35km (21 miles) until it reaches the river where the Linyanti entrance gate is. The camp site is about 5km (3 miles) beyond the gate.

◄ *Opposite: The rare and fascinating Pel's fishing owl.*
▼ *Below: A log bridge over the Savuti Channel.*

## THE BAD-TEMPERED BUFFALO

Many people consider buffalo (*Syncerus caffer*) to be just wild cows, in the same league as the Asian water buffalo, but nothing could be further from the truth. Along with leopard, many experienced game guides consider buffalo to be one the most dangerous animals in the bush. A fully grown male can weigh up to 800kg (almost 1800lb), and will stand just under 1.5m (5ft) at the shoulder. Dense bush and thickets should be avoided as bad-tempered bulls are often encountered in these confines.

▼ *Below: The buffalo is a formidable creature and is considered to be one of the most dangerous animals in the African bush.*

## KAZUNGULA ★★

This small riverine village is named after a huge sausage tree (*Kigelia africana*) – 'Mzungula' in the local tongue – which until recently could still be seen growing on the river bank overlooking the confluence of the Zambezi and Chobe rivers. The tree was made famous in the diaries of David Livingstone who camped beneath it in 1855, the night before he discovered the Victoria Falls. This settlement, situated in the furthest northeastern corner of Botswana, has grown up around the border post and the old river ferry mainly in order to service the needs of travellers and tourists passing through.

Basic supplies are available at Kazungula including petrol. Accommodation and camping facilities can be found at Kubu Lodge on the edge of the village towards Kasane from where boat trips to both the confluence or Chobe National Park can be arranged. Halfway along the 12km (7-mile) road to Kasane are banana plantations, and opposite them towards the river is a noticeably barren patch of land ringed by dead trees. This is a salt seep whose mineral-rich springs attract both elephants and buffalo. Many people are likewise attracted to the Kasane Hot Spring spa, but more for relaxing in the pools than for drinking the water.

There is a good tarred road to Nata, 320km (192 miles) away through dense stands of forest. As the unfenced boundary of Zimbabwe's Hwange National Park is a short distance to the east of the main road for much of the way between Pandamatenga and Kazungula, there is a good chance of seeing roan antelope, giraffe and elephant. Kazungula is Botswana's only border with Zambia and an old vehicle ferry currently shuttles between the two countries. But the governments of Botswana and Zambia have agreed that they will construct a US\$ 260 million bridge over the waterway to better link their countries. Construction is hoped to start in mid-2013.

At Kazungula travellers can cross into Zimbabwe to visit the majestic Victoria Falls.

### VICTORIA FALLS ★★★

To witness the falls stretching across almost 2km (5600ft) of sheer basalt cliffs with water crashing down over 100m (328ft) into the chasm below is definitely an unforgettable experience.

The many activities at the Victoria Falls include **white-water rafting**, which is reputed to be one of the safest and most exciting grade five runs in the world, as well as one of the world's most dramatic **bungi jumps** off the Railway Bridge into the churning 'boiling pot' a couple of hundred metres below.

▲ *Above: Sunrise over the spectacular main falls.*
▼ *Below: Bungi jumping: the fastest way into the boiling pot!*

### Routes to the Victoria Falls

A good route for day visitors from Botswana is to cross into Zambia on the car ferry from Kazungula and drive to the Victoria Falls via Livingstone, then leave your vehicle at the Mosi oa Tunya Hotel while exploring the Zambian side of the falls.

Having explored the Zambian side go through the Customs post and cross the original 1905 bridge that spans the neck of the second gorge which takes you into Zimbabwe. The paths through the dense rainforest lead from **Devil's Cataract** along the front of the falls, passing the **Main Falls**, **Horseshoe Falls**, **Rainbow Falls**, and finally to the open rocky platform at Danger Point.

There are numerous good hotels on both sides of the Falls where one can enjoy lunch, followed by a visit to the crocodile ranch or the Big Tree, a cruise up the Zambezi, a game drive or a round of golf at Elephant Hills before returning to Botswana.

Your passport and visas must be valid for Zimbabwe and Zambia and remember that the Kazungula border post now closes at 18:00 so you must leave the Falls by 16:30.

# CHOBE NATIONAL PARK AT A GLANCE

## Best Times to Visit

The **game viewing** throughout the Chobe improves as the pans dry up and the game concentrates around the permanent water sources such as the river or the pumped water holes, with **August** to **October** being considered the best times to visit. Game viewing is good along the Chobe riverfront throughout the year, but the Mababe Depression and the Savuti Channel are usually very difficult to access or closed during the **wettest months** from **December** to **March**. The summers can be uncomfortably hot, while in winter the early mornings, particularly in Savuti can be very cold. Strong **winds** often sweep across the Nogatsaa area in **August** and **September**.

## Getting There

There is an international airport at Kasane with regular **Air Botswana** flights from Gaborone, Francistown and Johannesburg. There are landing strips at both Savuti and Linyanti which service the private camps in those areas. There is a good tar road to Kasane from Francistown, while there are four-wheel-drive only routes to Savuti from Maun via Moremi. From Zimbabwe and Zambia the best route is via Kazungula, while from Namibia entry is via Katima Mulilo at the Ngoma Bridge border post. There is no rail link to Kasane, although there is an exclusive **Blue Train** rail safari that occasionally incorporates Chobe. It drops passengers off at the Victoria Falls; they are then flown to Kasane and, after a round of game drives, fly to Francistown where they reboard the train which returns to Johannesburg in South Africa.

## Getting Around

There are numerous safari operators in Kasane and all the lodges are able to arrange airport collections, game drives and boat trips for both guests and casual visitors. For those who prefer unguided trips, there is an **Avis** Rent-a-Car office at Kasane Airport, tel: 625 0144, fax: 625 0145, from where appropriate four-wheel-drive vehicles can be hired. Pre-booking of Avis vehicles can be done through any international travel agent.

## Where to Stay

There are many excellent lodges, hotels and luxury camps in the Chobe area, and with the concession system of land allocation for tourism operators in Botswana, new ones are being established all the time, so it is important to consult your travel agent who can recommend options that will suit your needs, wants and budget.

*Kasane*
**Chobe Marina Lodge**, tel: 625 2221, e-mail: res1@ chobemarinalodge.com In a beautiful setting on the banks of the Chobe river.
**Chobe Safari Lodge**, tel: 625 0336, e-mail: reservations@ chobesafarilodge.com Luxurious accommodation including camping, plus a restaurant, pool and shops.
**Mowana Safari Lodge**, tel: 625 0300, e-mail: resmowana@ cresta.co.bw Stunning architecture and setting with over 110 rooms and a choice of restaurants.
**The Garden Lodge**, tel: 625 0051, e-mail: reservations@ oshaughnessys.com Idyllic setting with very good accommodation, restaurant.
**Water Lily Lodge**, tel: 625 1775, e-mail: waterlily@ botsnet.bw Small, homely and good value with 10-room lodge facing garden and river.

*Kazungula*
**Bonazazi Border Lodge**, tel: 625 2999, e-mail: bonazazilodge@botsnet.bw Budget lodge where boat or game trips can be arranged.
**Kubu Lodge**, tel: 625 0312, e-mail: kubu@botsnet.bw Famous for its restaurant and wooden cabins set in lush lawn on the river bank, plus well serviced camp sites.
**Toro Safari Lodge**, tel: 625 2694, e-mail: torolodge@ botsnet.bw At the river confluence, offering a range of activities.

### Serondela
**Chobe Chilwero Sanctuary Retreat**, tel: 625 1362, e-mail: southernafrica@sanctuaryretreats.com Beautiful river views, outstanding food and attentive highly qualified game guides.
**Chobe Game Lodge**, tel: 625 0340 or 625 1761, e-mail: reservations@desertdelta.com Long established five-star luxury hotel with excellent facilities and game activities.

### Savuti
**Savuti Bush Camp**, tel: 686 0086, fax: 686 0632, e-mail: enquiry@wilderness.co.bw Five-star luxury on the Linyanti side of Savuti.
**Savuti Elephant Camp**, tel: +27 21 483 1600, e-mail: sandy.fowler@orient-express.com Stunning five-star lodge on the banks of the Savuti Channel overlooking a water hole.
**Savuti Safari Lodge**, tel: 686 1243, fax: 686 1791, e-mail: reception@dds.co.bw Luxurious game lodge offering excellent cuisine, game drives and river cruises.

### Linyanti
**Duma Tau Camp**, tel: +27 11 807 1800, e-mail: enquiry@wilderness.co.bw Luxury camp rebuilt near the source of the Savuti River.
**Kings Pool Camp**, same contact details as Duma Tau above. Luxurious five-star tented suites overlooking Kings Pool. Night drives and boat trips on offer.

**Selinda Reserve**, tel: 625 0505, e-mail: dorian.hoy@selindareserve.com Three luxury camps in the 300,000-acre reserve with excellent food, great guides and amazing settings.

### Lesoma
**Elephant Valley Lodge**, tel: 620 0054, e-mail: elephantvalley@yahoo.com Luxury tents set in dense pristine forest.
**Lesoma Valley Lodge**, tel: 625 1212, e-mail: lesomavalley@brobemail.co.bw Affordable accommodation is available in the Kasane forestry reserve 20km (12 miles) from Kasane.

### Ngoma
**Boabab 1 & 2 Safari Lodges**, tel: 686 0086, e-mail: reservations@wilderness.co.bw Facilities include boat cruises, game drives a restaurant and swimming pool.
**Muchenje Safari Lodge**, tel: 620 0013/4/5, e-mail: info@muchenje.com Four-star luxury offering game drives, fishing and walking safaris.

### Camping
There are three National Parks public camp sites in

the Chobe National Park; at **Ihaha** there are hot showers just 15km (9 miles) from Kasane; at **Savuti** where there are special 'elephant-proof' water points and showers; while at Linyanti the camp sites and ablution blocks are in a beautiful shady forest setting. There is also a privately owned camp site at **Buffalo Ridge** near Ngoma Gate which has running water and ablution facilities, while there is a wide choice of camp sites at the lodges in **Kasane** and **Kazungula**.

## WHERE TO EAT

Almost all of the above lodges and camps have restaurants offering excellent cuisine, although most are closed to the public (open to residents only). Public restaurants are only available in Kasane, Kazungula and Ngoma, and there are many.

## TOURS AND EXCURSIONS

All of the private lodges and camps offer their own game drives as well as boat trips (depending on their location). Public trips from Kasane can be arranged through any of the reputable travel agents.

| KASANE | J | F | M | A | M | J | J | A | S | O | N | D |
|---|---|---|---|---|---|---|---|---|---|---|---|---|
| MIN AVE TEMP. °C | 20 | 19 | 19 | 17 | 14 | 11 | 10 | 13 | 17 | 20 | 21 | 20 |
| MIN AVE TEMP. °F | 68 | 66 | 66 | 63 | 57 | 52 | 50 | 55 | 63 | 68 | 70 | 68 |
| MAX AVE TEMP. °C | 31 | 30 | 31 | 31 | 29 | 26 | 26 | 30 | 33 | 34 | 34 | 31 |
| MAX AVE TEMP. °F | 88 | 86 | 88 | 88 | 84 | 79 | 79 | 86 | 91 | 93 | 93 | 88 |
| RAINFALL mm | 141 | 138 | 71 | 19 | 1 | 0 | 0 | 0 | 1 | 28 | 51 | 142 |
| RAINFALL in | 5.6 | 5.4 | 2.8 | 0.7 | 0 | 0 | 0 | 0 | 0 | 1.1 | 2 | 5.6 |

# 8
# The Okavango Delta

As the world's largest inland delta, the Okavango covers over 15,000km² (5700 sq miles) of lush verdant wetland. This unique area contains an incredible 95% of all surface water in Botswana and is one of Africa's prime tourist destinations. Surrounded by the parched Kalahari, this emerald jewel is an immense oasis fed by the flow of the mighty Okavango River which, unlike every other major river in the world, never reaches the sea but dies in the desert sands of northern Botswana.

The Delta is roughly cone-shaped and is approximately 175km (110 miles) in length from the apex to its base near Maun. It has given rise to a teeming variety of life, sustained by a myriad seasonally undulating waterways which provide an ideal environment for the plants and animals of the Okavango.

This remarkable region has been recognized by the RAMSAR Convention as a 'Wetland of International Importance' and as of 2014 it will – finally – be a fully protected UNESCO World Heritage Site. In a comparison to seven other globally important wetlands, UNESCO has concluded that the Okavango 'has the highest number of reptile and bird species, second highest number of plant and mammal species and third highest number of fish species. Moremi Game Reserve within the Okavango Delta has some of the highest different animal species populations in southern Africa, which is comparable with the rich savannas in the East African Rift Valley.' Little wonder the Okavango Delta is the crowning glory of Botswana's entire tourism industry.

## DON'T MISS

*** A relaxing **mokoro ride** across the lagoons.
*** A **game viewing flight** over submerged flood plains.
*** **Exploring** hidden, uninhabited islands deep in the Delta.
*** **Casting** your line into the boiling waters of the annual **catfish run**.
** Sighting the rare aquatic **sitatunga** and **red lechwe**.

◀ *Opposite: A mokoro drifts lazily through the water lilies of the Santadadibe River, deep in the Okavango wetlands.*

# THE OKAVANGO DELTA

The Okavango has a long dry winter from May to October with little or no rainfall. The days are warm and often cloudless, although the nights and early morning can be cold with temperatures near freezing. The majority of rain falls between December and February, and from November to April it can be oppressively hot and humid.

## MAUN

Almost all tourists entering the Okavango do so through Maun, situated at the gateway to the Delta and Moremi Game Reserve. Maun is the tourism capital of Botswana and the administrative centre of Ngamiland. It is also the headquarters of countless safari and air-charter operations whose signs and offices dot almost every intersection, particularly towards the airport.

Since the town's establishment in 1915 as the tribal capital of the Batawana people, Maun has had a rough and ready reputation as a hard-living 'Wild West' town servicing the local cattle-ranching and hunting

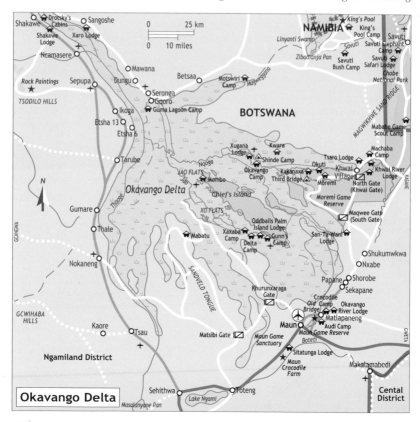

Okavango Delta

operations. But with the growth of the tourism industry and the completion of the tar road from Francistown in the early 1990s, Maun has developed rapidly, losing much of its old frontier town character. It is now the tourism capital of Botswana and home to almost 56,000 people, nearly three-quarters of whom make their livelihoods from tourism.

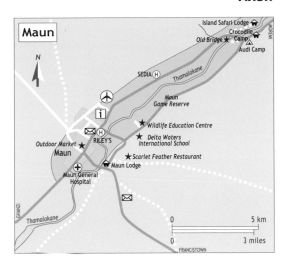

Regular supplies of almost everything can be bought in Maun, and the town boasts several shopping centres, filling stations, a choice of hotels and lodges as well as car and four-wheel-drive vehicle hire. With all the charter traffic that uses Maun airport, it is the busiest in Botswana.

The name Maun is derived from the San word *maung* which means 'the place of short reeds' and this metropolis is now spread out along the wide banks of the timeless Thamalakane River where red lechwe can still be seen grazing next to local donkeys, goats and cattle.

Other areas of interest in and around Maun include the small **Maun Game Reserve** which covers just 8km² (2.4 sq miles) of woodland. It follows the Thamalakane river bank upstream from Riley's Hotel and includes the original 'Place of Reeds' from which the town takes its name. The reserve is open every day and is traversed by numerous walking trails for which a small entrance fee is charged.

### Maun Crocodile Farm ★★

The Maun Crocodile Farm, situated near Sitatunga Camp southwest of Maun, has hundreds of crocodiles penned in near-natural surroundings. The farm offers daily guided tours.

---

**FACTS AND FIGURES OF THE OKAVANGO**

**Total river length** – 1430km (872 miles).
**Average sediment load** – 650,000 tons per year.
**Delta size** – 15,846km² (6038 sq miles).
**Delta composition:**
**Perennial wetlands** – 4887km² (1862 sq miles);
**Seasonal wetlands** – 3855km² (1470 sq miles);
**Seasonal grassland** – 2760km² (1052 sq miles);
**Intermittent flooding** – 2502km² (954 sq miles)
**Dry land** – 1842km² (702 sq miles).

▲ *Above: Modern Maun: the 'Place of Reeds' on the far left, Riley's Hotel in the trees and the commercial centre in the distance.*
▶ *Opposite: Moremi Game Reserve's north entrance.*

## THE SEASONAL FLOOD

The oscillating flow of water across the Okavango Delta is a timeless constant of rejuvenation and regeneration, peaking in the parched southern reaches in the dry winter months. The reason for this abundance of water in what is usually the dry season is the distant rainfall in Angola; it takes the floodwater a full six months to wash through the Delta. It reaches the Panhandle in May, but slows down in the flat sandy-bottomed Delta until the meagre unevaporated remains reach Maun, usually some time in August. The arrival of the waters in Maun is greeted with much local excitement and every year bets are made as to the exact time and date of its arrival.

## Nhabe Museum **

The Nhabe Museum is housed in an historic military building used by the British as a surveillance post against the Germans during World War II. It is on the main road near the airport. In addition, there are curio and craft shops, including the Bushman Craft Shop near the airport, the Leopard's Lair opposite the runway, Thuso Curio Shop off the Toteng road and Mukwa Woodcraft, at the Mukwa Leaf Gardens near the Sedia Hotel. Open 08:00–17:00 Monday–Friday, 11:00–16:00 Saturday.

## Matlapaneng Bridge **

Just outside Maun on the road to Moremi, near the turn-off to Crocodile Camp and Island Safari Lodge is the old Matlapaneng Bridge, which has been preserved as a National Monument. Going out of town take the dirt track to the right just before the new bridge and you'll cross the ancient calcrete and mopane pole bridge. There is a pleasant picnic site on the eastern side of the bridge next to the water hole. Local legend has it that this water hole is bottomless as it never dries up and hippos and crocodiles seem to unexpectedly come up from its depths. Over the decades many unlicensed firearms have been dispatched into this muddy abyss.

There are many different people living in Maun from the Batawana and the Bayei, to the Basubiya, Hambukushu and the Mbanderu group of the Herero people. This distinctive group of Herero live near the centre of Maun at the turn-off to the old single-lane bridge, where you are bound to see the flamboyantly dressed women in their flowing Victorian outfits. If you are tempted to take their photograph, it is important to ask permission first and to pay the women a fee for the imposition.

The Francistown to Maun road is 492km (306 miles) of good tar, as is now the road from Ghanzi to Maun. This 286km (173-mile) stretch was tarred in the early 2000s, finally completing the circular road around Botswana.

## MOREMI GAME RESERVE ★★★

Moremi boasts one of the richest and most diverse ecosystems on the continent, being described as one of the most beautiful game reserves in Africa – if not the whole world. As if these accolades are not enough, the prestigious African Travel and Tourism Association has voted Moremi 'the best game reserve in Africa.'

It is here that land and water meet in a perfect balance of stunningly beautiful flood plains, lagoons, pools and pans, all edged in lush green riverine forest and tall tropical palm trees. This verdant oasis is home to not just the Big Five, but almost every African creature you could ever hope to see.

Originally proclaimed by the tribe who lived in the area back in 1963, Moremi was the very first reserve in Africa established by the local residents. It is named after their leader, Chief Moremi III.

Covering 4872km² (1856 sq miles) Moremi is only accessible by air or four-wheel-drive vehicle, and only the eastern side of the reserve is accessible by road as much of the central and all of the western side of the park consists of dense swampland. In the wet season many of the roads become impassable.

There are several private lodges along the park boundary, but within Moremi there are only four public camp sites.

### WHERE THE WATER GOES

The huge mass of water in the Okavango Delta represents 95% of all surface water in Botswana, but with a giant surface area, shallow depths and high daytime temperatures, 96% of it is lost to evaporation, 2% is absorbed into the underground water table while a mere 2% drains into the Thamalakane River. With water being such a scarce and valuable resource, in Botswana there have been many utilization plans to tap the Okavango's waters, while others in Angola and Namibia also claim rights to the water. However, environmentalists have proven that even a fractional reduction in the average flow will cause the destruction of unique flora and fauna in the southern flood plains. Both the International Union for the Conservation of Nature (IUCN) and Green Peace have studied the sensitive ecology of the Delta and have been instrumental in the successful lobbying for this wetland to be declared a World Heritage Site.

### South Gate Camp Site ★★

This camp site is set in a clean open, but grassless area under tall mopane trees, right at the **Maqwee Gate**. With a couple of ablution blocks equipped with boilers for hot water, it is an ideal site for those arriving at the gate late in the afternoon who would be unable to reach any of the other sites before the closing time when driving is no longer permitted.

# THE OKAVANGO DELTA

### GUARDIANS OF THE DELTA

Tsetse fly (*Glossina morsitans*) are endemic to the Delta and, as the carrier of both the feared **African sleeping sickness** in humans and foot-and-mouth disease in cattle, there have been numerous attempts to exterminate these parasites, including slaughtering all the wildlife that provide a possible food source for the flies, chopping down all the acacia trees which provide shade for them, and, more recently the blanket aerial spraying of DDT over the entire Delta. None of these destructive methods has worked and now the Tsetse Fly Control Department has devised a more effective and environmentally friendly system of 'flag' traps. The numbers of these insects are now greatly reduced but if you are nipped be thankful that they are still there to stall the encroachment of the hungry herds of cattle.

▶ Right: The fearsome crocodiles found in the Delta can grow up to 6m (19ft) in length and weigh over a tonne.

### Third Bridge Camp Site ★★★

The popular Third Bridge Camp Site is situated 55km (34 miles) northwest of Maqwee Gate. Approximately 43km (27 miles) from Maqwee the road crosses two old rickety mopane pole bridges which are predictably known as First Bridge and Second Bridge, and are the crossing point onto **Mboma Island**. Third Bridge and its adjacent camp site are a further 12km (7 miles) along the main track. The site is shady and idyllically situated on the edge of a permanent, clear lagoon. This clean water is safe to drink but do not consider swimming as there have been attacks by **crocodiles**.

The site includes barbecue stands and ablution blocks with hot showers – although you may have to light the boiler fires to heat the water. Be warned that Third Bridge is renowned for its lions which use the bridge and walk through the camp at night, so do not camp too near the bridge and don't wander about in the dark.

**Fourth Bridge** is 6km (3½ miles) beyond Third Bridge and is near a series of pools and pans, including **Botelele Pool** which attracts vast numbers of animals and birds and has its own resident hippos and some big crocodiles. The **Dobetsaa Pans** are to the south of the bridge and are one of the few places in the park where one is likely to see the remarkable **African skimmer**. Pelicans are sometimes seen at **Maya Pan** on the way to Xakanaxa.

### Xakanaxa Lagoon ***

Xakanaxa Lagoon, 42km (26 miles) northwest of South Gate, boasts some of the widest varieties of fish to be found anywhere in the Delta. It is some 12km (7 miles) north of Fourth Bridge and is a vast expanse of deep, permanent reed-lined waterways. Several private camps and lodges have been established along the edge of the lagoon including **Camp Moremi** and **Camp Okuti**. Just outside these lodges is a small shop selling basic provisions. This is the only area in Moremi where boats and canoes can be hired.

▲ *Above: Real fan palms silhouetted against the setting sun.*

### Xakanaxa Camp Site **

Xakanaxa Camp Site is just after the lodges, spread out on a thin strip of dry land between the Xakanaxa lagoon and a dense wetland reedbed. The site has ablution blocks with hot showers and a slipway to launch boats.

### Nyandambesi Lediba and Dombo Hippo Pool ***

It is a long journey of almost 45km (27 miles) from Xakanaxa to North Gate where the fourth camp site is located. This route is flood-prone so check conditions before you set off. It is worth breaking this trip with a visit to **Nyandambesi Lediba** and the **Dombo Hippo Pool** on the way. Nyandambesi Lediba, which means 'the lagoon where you can barbecue catfish', is an open series of pools and is less than 10km (6 miles) from the Xakanaxa camp site. At Dombo Hippo Pool, which is the site of the old village of the Bugakhwe people, there is a large resident herd of hippos, usually accompanied by crocodiles, lechwe and a flotilla of water birds. There is an observation hide which is signposted and which can be found a short distance off the main Xakanaxa/Khwai road, some 12km (7 miles) from Khwai.

## DRIVING TIMES

In 1996 the Department of Wildlife and National Parks extended the park opening hours, which used to be effectively from sunrise to sunset. They now open just before dawn and extend into the first hour of nightfall. This enables campers to enjoy the sunset at a nearby spot before setting off back to camp, and also to have a better chance of catching glimpses of the rarely seen nocturnal birds and animals. For the exact opening and closing times, see the chart in the Travel Tips section on page 122.

### North Gate Camp Site **

North Gate camp site, some 30km (18 miles) north of Maqwee, is situated under shady trees directly after the North Gate bridge on the banks of the river opposite Khwai village. This 'bridge over the river Khwai' is a long picturesque structure made entirely of rattly mopane poles. The usual camping facilities are here, while there are one or two small rural stores in Khwai village selling only the most basic commodities. Be aware that the monkeys in Khwai will steal anything they can from the moment you arrive. Therefore ensure that your tents and vehicle windows are closed at all times.

There are several lodges and camps in the Khwai area on the northern river bank outside the game reserve, such as **Tsaro Lodge**, the famous **Khwai River Lodge**, and **Machaba Camp** which is further along the Chobe road. All offer excellent game drives into the area. Khwai is well known for its concentrations of **elephant** and large herds of them can be seen towards the late afternoon heading down to the river. All of the loop roads that skirt the river banks offer the chance of rewarding elephant sightings.

### Routes into Moremi

From the 'Bridge over the River Khwai' it is just 22km (13.5 miles) to the Chobe National Park boundary. For those going back to Maun there is a direct road from Khwai to Maqwee which cuts straight across the mopane woodlands for 30km (18 miles), but this road is challenging in the wet summer months.

There are **airstrips** at both Khwai and Xakanaxa, but most visitors to Moremi drive in from either Maun or Savuti. From **Maun** the road is tarred up to the village of **Shorobe**. There are a few little shops in this village, but no petrol, and from here the road is gravel for the next 11km (7 miles) up to

▼ *Below: Tourists in a mokoro glide quietly across the waters.*

◄ Left: Red lechwe graze near the edge of a palm-lined waterway.

the Buffalo fence. This is the boundary to the wildlife management area that surrounds Moremi and the road degenerates dramatically from here onwards, making four-wheel-drive essential. A short distance beyond the Buffalo fence the road forks. **Maqwee Gate** into Moremi is 34km (21 miles) from this junction on the left-hand fork, while the right-hand fork is the road leading to Savuti and Kasane. One should allow around three hours to complete the 98km (60-mile) journey from Maun to South Gate.

### The Bukakhwe San Bushmen's Gudigwa Camp ★★★
In the early 2000s one of southern Africa's most ancient and vulnerable communities, the Bukakhwe San Bushmen with the help of Conservation International and Okavango Wilderness Safaris established Gudigwa Camp. Through walking tours this unique community-run ecotourism project teaches guests about the ancient San cultural heritage including the use of medicinal plants, gathering water in the dry season, traditional storytelling, song and dance.

## THE CENTRAL AND SOUTHERN OKAVANGO
The permanently and seasonally flooded areas within the central and southern Okavango hide within their cloak of beautiful lagoons, backwaters and forested islands some of the finest safari camps in the world.

**WHY THE HIPPO SCATTERS HIS DUNG**

You will notice that both on land and in water hippos have a strange habit of scattering their dung with their tails. Local legend has it that when the world was young the hippo asked God if he could live in the lovely cool water. But God said no, because he was so big with such a huge mouth he would eat up all the fish. The hippo pleaded with God saying that he would never harm the fish and that he just wanted to be nice and cool. Eventually they agreed that the hippo could live in the water, but that he must scatter his dung so that from heaven, God can look down to see that there are no fish bones in it, just pure grass.

# THE OKAVANGO DELTA

▶ Right: Guests enjoy a sumptuous dinner after their evening game drive at one of the Delta's luxury camps.

Down the length of the Delta these safari camps offer visitors a range of activities. The northern and central camps tend to concentrate on aquatic activities such as fishing and mokoro safaris, while the southern camps offer terrestrial activities, such as game drives and walks.

Some camps outside the Moremi National Park boundary offer **night boat rides** to see the crocodiles and birds. The eyes of the crocodiles are highly reflective and it is terrifying to see just how many there are out there.

## THE PANHANDLE, TSODILO AND WESTERN OKAVANGO

Known as the Cubango, the **Okavango River** rises in the rain-drenched Bie Plateau in northeastern Angola. From here it flows south across 1300km (800 miles) of Kalahari sand before changing its name to the Okavango when it enters Botswana at Mohembo.

The Okavango River flows between two parallel faults which form a shallow valley just over 10km (7 miles) wide. Within this constriction, aptly known as the **Panhandle**, the river flows straight for 95km (59 miles). Then just beyond the tiny village of Seronga on its northeastern bank, the river crosses the **Gomare Fault**, which releases it to spill its waters into the huge Delta.

### Shakawe ★★★
Since the early 1990s, the Panhandle has become more accessible with the tarring of the Maun/Shakawe road and with the establishment of numerous camps and lodges along the riverbank.

◀ Left: A walking safari led by a game guide wades through the shallow water between two islands.

With the Panhandle being deep and fast-flowing it is ideal for sports fishing. Seventeen species of fish can be caught here, and they are all prized by anglers. Bird-watching is also outstanding in the tall, shady riverine forests, and many resident and migratory birds can be seen along the river.

A visit to the Panhandle would not be complete without an excursion to the Tsodilo Hills, and most of the camps in the Shakawe and Panhandle area can arrange either fly-in or four-wheel-drive day or overnight excursions to this incredible archeological gallery.

### Tsodilo Hills ★★★

Tsodilo, just west of the Okavango River Panhandle, is a mystical place of incredible historic, cultural and spiritual importance. This UNESCO World Heritage Site has been occupied almost continually for the last 100,000 years, and over the last 20,000 the San people decorated the honey-toned granite panels of Tsodilo with more than 4500 individual paintings, making this one of the most important rock art sites in the world. These world-famous paintings include remarkable images of animals, human figures and geometric patterns. In addition to rhino, eland and giraffe, there are also very unusual 'whale' and 'penguin' images which defy logic.

There are four hills at Tsodilo. The tallest is the Male Hill. It reaches up 410m (1345ft) above the plain, and at 1400m (4595ft) above sea level it is the second highest point in Botswana, on which the Hambukushu people

## BE CONSIDERATE

If you are taking part in night excursions, please be sensitive to the wildlife and appreciate that the intrusion of a blinding spotlight can be very disturbing, especially to some of the sleeping birds who may take hours to find a suitable perch again once you have gone. Also don't encourage your boatman to feed the wildlife, especially the fish eagles. It is a dramatic thing to watch one of these powerful birds scooping a fish out of the water and many unthinking tourists like to try their hand at photographing these staged events, but the birds become dependant and overfeed, ultimately leading to their demise.

believe that God created mankind. Next to it is the 300m (985ft) Female Hill, where San legend has it that the Gods of Old live in caverns deep within the hill. The most terrifying of these gods is a giant serpent, with huge spiralling horns, that occupies a dark subterranean lake.

The road to Tsodilo is west off the main Maun to Shakawe road, 32km (20 miles) south of Shakawe. Although sandy and corrugated it is usually well graded. But when you get to Tsodilo all the tracks around the hills are deep sand and you need four-wheel-drive to get to the four beautifully located camp sites. There is a small museum at Tsodilo, and the camp site next to it even has ablutions and running water.

### Drotsky's Caves and the Gcwihaba and Aha Hills **

These attractions are extremely remote and difficult to reach, making them challenges for only the most adventurous. The magnificent chambers of these only partially explored caves, the name of which means 'Hyena's hole', are reputed to hide within them Hendrik van Zyl's lost treasure. But if you visit them, be careful not to lose yourself within the maze of passages and wondrous formations. Take the turning to Xaixai 1.5km (1 mile) west of Tsau. After 93km (58 miles), turn left down a track signposted 'Xhaba Borehole'. The Gcwihaba Hills and the entrance to Drotsky's Caves is 54km (34 miles) down this track. Shady trees provide good camping, but be prepared for a significant camping fee – and they only take cash.

To get to the Aha Hills, continue west on the same track for another 27km (17 miles) until you rejoin the Xaixai road 10km (6 miles) before the village. The Aha Hills are 10km (6 miles) north of Xaixai.

### Etsha 6 ***

There are several small villages on the main Maun/ Shakawe road, some of which were settled by Hambu-

▼ *Below: The bastion of the Tsodilo Hills towers over the surrounding plain.*

◀ *Left: Papyrus fires are a common phenomenon in the delta, with the peat banks bursting into flame at the slightest disturbance.*

## SAN PLACE NAMES

Many place names in Moremi are of San origin; the sounds of this **San language** are difficult to pronounce:
**x** – a click, formed by sealing the tongue against the roof of the mouth and then sucking it down loudly.
**q** – made by pulling the tongue loudly away from the back of the front teeth.
**xhl** or **//** – produced by pressing the tongue against the teeth as if pronouncing the letter 'l', but instead, air is sucked in and the 'click' is pronounced at the back of the mouth, rather like the sound made to encourage a horse.

kushu refugees who fled the war in Angola in the late 1960s. These people brought with them the skill of weaving and this area is now the centre of Botswana's most important craft industry – basket weaving.

The village of **Etsha 6** is the largest of the 13 settlements of Etsha and lies 30km (19 miles) north of Gumare. It boasts a selection of shops and a filling station as well as the **Etsha Museum and Cultural Centre**. In Etsha 6 you will also find the **Okavango Basket Shop**. Open Monday–Saturday from 08:00–17:00. Just 14km (9 miles) away to the east, set in shady palms on the banks of an Okavango tributary is **Makwena Lodge**, making Etsha 6 an ideal overnight stop or holiday destination in itself.

### Lake Ngami *
Lake Ngami is a relic of the super-lake that once covered much of northern Botswana. Over the last few decades the lake had almost completely dried up, but with the record levels of flood water that drained out of the Okavango in 2011, Lake Ngami has refilled, now covering an area of almost 200km$^2$ (75 sq miles).

There are no camping facilities, plenty of mosquitoes, and many of the old roads are flooded. But the extremely nutritious water makes the lake rich in fish, which has brought back vast numbers of the water birds, including flamingoes and pelicans, for which it was once famous.

## SMOULDERING EARTH

Lake Ngami has always been a mysterious place surrounded by legends and strange phenomenon, such as the smouldering earth around the lake flats that the local inhabitants believe is caused by the angry god, Lengongoro. The cause of this strange inextinguishable fire has vexed many. The real reason seems to be the **spontaneous combustion** of the deeply packed reedbeds that burn for months beneath the surface until the rains and floodwaters extinguish them.

# THE OKAVANGO DELTA AT A GLANCE

## BEST TIMES TO VISIT

**Aug–Nov** is considered to be the best, as after the first rains (can be in late Nov), the game rapidly disperses. Summer can be very hot but many of the animals have young which can provide fascinating viewing.

## GETTING THERE

There are regular flights to Maun from Gaborone, Victoria Falls, South Africa and Namibia. All the camps in the Delta organize charter flights for their guests and these are usually frequent and timed to the Air Botswana arrivals. Some southern camps can be reached by boat, but with the papyrus obstructions and fluctuating water levels this needs to be arranged in advance. Few camps in the Delta can be reached by road, save for the camps in Moremi, Shakawe and along the western edge of the Okavango. Four-wheel-drive is essential off the main Maun–Shakawe road. Roads from Francistown, Ghanzi and Shakawe are all good tar. The road on the eastern edge of the Okavango is very sandy and difficult even in four-wheel-drive.

## GETTING AROUND

The roads within Moremi are navigable by four-wheel-drive only and some are seasonal and may be submerged. Most camps in the Delta offer game drives and mokoro rides. While mekoro are the most common means of transport in the central and southern Delta, they are not recommended in the Pan-handle where the river is fast flowing and crocodile infested. In this area stick to conventional boats.

## WHERE TO STAY

There are many camps and lodges within the Okavango area with new ones being established all the time. Most camps are on land concessions that are not automatically renewed so they may be relocated. Hence use the following as a guide-line only – check with your travel agent.

### Maun
**Audi Camp**, 13km (8 miles) out of town on the Moremi road, tel: 686 0599, e-mail: audicamp@info.bw Camp site with a bar, restaurant and pool.
**Crocodile Camp**, tel: 680 0222, e-mail: sales@crocodilecamp.com Excellent restaurant and pool on the bank of the Thamalakane river near Audi Camp.
**Cresta Rileys Hotel**, tel: 686 0204, e-mail: resrileys@cresta.co.bw In centre of town, good restaurant and atmospheric Harry's Bar.
**Maun Lodge**, tel: 686 3939, e-mail: maun.lodge@info.bw Fully serviced hotel on the banks of the Thamalakane river, with good restaurant, boma and famous Pygmy Goose cocktail bar.

**Sedia Riverside Hotel**, tel: 686 0177, e-mail: sedia@info.bw Comfortable hotel on Shorobe Road.

### Central Okavango
**Guma Lagoon Camp**, tel: 687 4626, e-mail: info@guma-lagoon.com Overlooking the lagoon; fishing, bird-watching, boating and walking.
**Jao Camp**, tel: 686 0086, e-mail: enquiry@wilderness.co.bw Five-star exclusive island camp, including gymnasium.
**Mombo Camp**, same contact details as Jao Camp above. This world-famous luxury camp is situated in the heart of the Delta.
**Xugana Island Lodge**, tel: 686 1243, e-mail: info@desertdelta.com Reed and thatch chalets on stilts; game viewing, mokoro safaris.

### Eastern Okavango
**Gudigwa Bukakhwe Cultural Village**, tel: 718 43657, e-mail: enquiry@gudigwa.com This is a unique eco-tourism experience with grass shelters in a genuine San environment.
**Khwai River Lodge**, tel: +27 11 274 1800, e-mail: sandy.fowler@orient-express.com Luxurious lodge overlooking the flood plain of the River Khwai.
**Shinde Camp**, tel: 686 0375, e-mail: info@kerdowney.bw Exclusive camp specializing in walking and mokoro safaris.

*Southern Okavango*
**Abu's Camp and Private Villa**, tel: 686 1260, e-mail: ebs@info.bw Famous for their elephant-back safaris.
**Eagle Island Camp**, tel: +27 11 274 1800, e-mail: sandy.fowler@orient-express.com Five-star luxury in one of the delta's most beautiful locations.
**Gunn's Camp**, tel: 686 4436, e-mail: reservations@gunns-camp.com Famous tented camp 'deep in the Delta'.
**Oddballs Palm Island Lodge,** tel: 686 1154, e-mail: info@lodgesofbotswana.com Island lodge offering mokoro and walking safaris.

*Moremi Game Reserve*
**Camp Moremi**, tel: 686 1243, e-mail: info@desertdelta.com This luxury camp offers excellent cuisine and game viewing.
**Camp Okuti**, tel: 686 0375, e-mail: info@kerdowney.bw 'A special African experience' at Xakanaxa lagoon.
**Santawani Lodge**, tel: 680 0664, e-mail: operationsstw@botsnet.bw Affordable accommodation that benefits nearby Sankuyu Village.

*Shakawe*
**Drotsky's Cabins**, tel: 687 5043, e-mail: drotskys@info.bw Breathtakingly beautiful riverside setting.
**Shakawe Lodge**, tel: 686 0820, e-mail: win@travelwild.co.bw On the banks of the river 25km (15 miles) from the Namibian border.

*Camping*
Department of Wildlife and National Parks camp sites are at South Gate, Third Bridge, Xakanaxa and Khwai. All these sites have basic facilities including showers and boilers for hot water. Book in advance at the Maun office, tel: 686 1265, fax: 686 1264.

## WHERE TO EAT

The Delta camps serve outstanding cuisine, but are generally closed to the public. But there are good restaurants and take-aways in Maun and the nearby lodges, including:
**French Connection**, tel: 680 0625. European cuisine.
**Sports Bar & Restaurant**, tel: 686 2676. Buzzing action bar and diner.
**Hilary's**, tel: 686 1610. Very popular, serving genuine home cooking.

## TOURS AND EXCURSIONS

Travel agents and tour operators organize tours to almost anywhere in the Okavango, including elephant-back and horse-back safaris, helicopter tours and mokoro trails. For fishing safaris contact Okavango Fishing Safaris in Shakawe, tel: 687 5092.

## USEFUL CONTACTS

**Parks and Reserves** reservations can be made at their head office, tel: 686 1265, fax: 686 1264.
**Avis Rent-a-Car**, tel: 686 0039, e-mail: avismun@botsnet.bw
**Riley's Garage & Service Station**, tel: 686 0203, e-mail: parts@rileys.co.bw

*Safari Operators:*
**Abercrombie and Kent**, tel: 686 2688, e-mail: apost@sanctuaryretreats.com
**Ker and Downey**, tel: 686 0375, e-mail: info@kerdowney.bw
**Okavango Wilderness Safaris**, tel: 686 0086, e-mail: enquiry@wilderness.co.bw

*Air Charter Companies:*
**Mack Air**, tel: 686 0675, e-mail: reservations@mackair.co.bw
**Flying Mission Service**, tel: 686 1456, fax: 686 2109.
**Moremi Air Services**, tel: 686 3632, e-mail: info@moremiair.com
**Sefofane**, tel: 686 0778, e-mail: neill@sefofane.bw

| MAUN | J | F | M | A | M | J | J | A | S | O | N | D |
|---|---|---|---|---|---|---|---|---|---|---|---|---|
| MIN AVE TEMP. °C | 20 | 19 | 19 | 16 | 11 | 8 | 7 | 10 | 15 | 19 | 20 | 20 |
| MIN AVE TEMP. °F | 68 | 66 | 66 | 61 | 52 | 46 | 45 | 50 | 59 | 66 | 68 | 68 |
| MAX AVE TEMP. °C | 33 | 32 | 33 | 32 | 29 | 26 | 26 | 29 | 34 | 36 | 35 | 34 |
| MAX AVE TEMP. °F | 91 | 90 | 91 | 90 | 84 | 79 | 79 | 84 | 93 | 97 | 95 | 93 |
| RAINFALL mm | 112 | 105 | 62 | 27 | 3 | 1 | 0 | 0 | 5 | 19 | 48 | 82 |
| RAINFALL in | 4.4 | 4.1 | 2.4 | 1.1 | 0.1 | 0 | 0 | 0 | 0.2 | 0.7 | 1.9 | 3.2 |

# Travel Tips

## Tourist Information

All of Botswana's international embassies have tourism representatives from the **Ministry of Environment, Wildlife and Tourism**. They have large-scale maps and tourism directories available to the public. The Department's head office is in Gaborone's main Mall. For enquiries tel: 395 3024.

The **Department of Wildlife and National Parks** is responsible for the administration of all the national parks. Their head office is in Gaborone: PO Box 131, tel: 397 1405, fax: 391 2354. They also have an office in Maun, tel: 686 0368. Prepaid bookings for camping and entry into the northern parks must be made via this Maun office, and unbooked visitors will not be allowed in. For other camping bookings contact the Parks & Reserves Reservations (Gaborone), tel: 318 0774.

The **Hotel And Tourism Association of Botswana** (HATAB), tel: 395 7144, fax: 390 3201, e-mail: hatab@hatab.bw is a private organization with representatives from the tourism industry who promote the country in conjunction with the government.

There are several conservation societies and wildlife foundations in Botswana, such as: **Kalahari Conservation Society**, tel: 397 4557, e-mail: admin@kcs.org.bw Promotes the conservation of the country's natural resources.

**Chobe Wildlife Trust**, tel: 625 0516, e-mail: cwt@info.bw Aims to preserve the natural assets of the Chobe National Park and northern Botswana.

**The Botswana Society**, tel: 391 9745, e-mail: botsoc@info.bw Records the history and social development of the country.

**National Park** opening and closing times are:

| | |
|---|---|
| January | 05:30–19:00 |
| February | 05:30–19.00 |
| March | 05:30–19:00 |
| April | 06:00–18:30 |
| May | 06:00–18:30 |
| June | 06:00–18:30 |
| July | 06:00–18:30 |
| August | 06:00–18:30 |
| September | 06:00–18:30 |
| October | 05:30–19:00 |
| November | 05:30–19:00 |
| December | 05:30–19:00 |

## Entry Requirements

Visitors to Botswana must have a valid passport and visa if necessary. Visas are not required for holders of South African, US or EU passports. As regulations are subject to change, it is worth checking with any Botswana Embassy, Air Botswana or your travel agent if you will need a visa before you travel to Botswana.

## Health Requirements

While Botswana is not a risky place to visit, certain precautions should be taken. Malaria, bilharzia and AIDS are main concerns but can be easily avoided. Tourists entering Botswana from southern African or western countries do not require inoculations, but vaccination certificates are necessary if you have recently been to a yellow fever zone. Piped water in urban Botswana is safe to drink and most tourist lodges and camps have reliable supplies, especially in the Okavango where the water is fresh and clean. But in the rest of the country check before drinking the water and when in doubt, boil all water before drinking. Health insurance should be organized before arrival in Botswana, as most camps and operators do not automatically cover guests. Local medical rescue and evacuation cover is recommended – contact MRI Botswana, tel: 390 3066, fax: 316 4728, e-mail: enquiries@mri.co.bw

### Getting There

**By Air:** Most fly-in tourists initially land in Gaborone, although some also fly directly into Maun and Kasane. Pre-arranged charter flights can be made to most airstrips within the country, but an initial landing may have to be made at a larger airport where Customs and Immigration formalities can be cleared first.

**By Road:** There are almost 25 official crossing points into Botswana, from the busy Tlokweng border which is open 18 hours a day to the simple desk under the tree at the Chobe River mokoro taxi crossing. Road travellers usually enter at Tlokweng or Pioneer Gate from South Africa, Ramatlabama from Zimbabwe, Ngoma Bridge or Mamuno from Namibia, and Kazungula from Zambia.

**By Rail:** Travellers can get to Botswana by train, but the line only runs between Lobatse and Francistown, passing through Gaborone and the larger towns of the east, and does not link with any tourist destinations.

### Customs

Customs regulations are subject to change so please treat the following as a guide only

and confirm the current import limits before you arrive in Botswana with the Department of Customs & Excise (P/Bag 0013, Gaborone, tel: 363 8000, fax: 363 9999, e-mail: comms@burs.org.bw). Visitors are allowed to import 200 cigarettes, 20 cigars, 250g tobacco, 1 litre spirits, 2 litres wine and 50ml perfume. Botswana is part of the 100-year-old Southern African Customs Union with South Africa, Namibia, Lesotho and Swaziland which means that products imported from these countries are not subject to import duty (although sales tax may be charged on certain items). Imports from other countries are subject to customs duty. It is important to declare all valuable camera, optical and electronic equipment with the Customs upon arrival so that it can be easily taken out again with no questions about its origin. Hunting rifles can only be imported with a valid Police permit issued by the Central Arms Registry.

### Transport

**Road:** Although all the main centres in Botswana are now linked with good tar roads, the country still has a relatively limited road network which is still being developed. Secondary roads off these main arteries are generally gravel and mostly only suitable for four-wheel-drive vehicles. You may also find some primary roads in a poor state with potholes, especially after the rainy season. Four-wheel-drive is necessary in

### USEFUL SETSWANA PHRASES

Hello Sir/Madam • *Dumela Rra/Mma*
Hello gentlemen/ladies • *Dumelang borra/bomma*
How are you? • *Le kae?*
I am fine • *Ke teng*
Stay well • *Sala sentle* (said when you're leaving)
Travel well • *Tsamaya sentle* (said when someone else is leaving)
Sleep well • *Robala sentle*
Thank you • *Ke tumetse/tanki*
Okay/fine/goodbye • *Go siame*
Yes • *Ee*
No • *Nnyaa*
Petrol • *Lookwae/Peterolo*
Bread • *Borotho/Senkgwe*
Water • *Metsi*
I want to see the doctor • *Ke batla go bona ngaka*
How much does this cost? • *Ke bokae?*

almost all the national parks and game reserves in Botswana and these roads are not likely to be upgraded in the foreseeable future.

**Driver's Licence:** Always carry your original driver's licence and vehicle registration book with you. This is a legal requirement and if you cannot produce this paperwork you may face a long walk to fetch it!

**Road Rules:** In Botswana vehicles drive on the left and give way to the right, but take care as other drivers may not know this and can be unpredictable, especially minibus taxis which often stop in unexpected places. The general speed limit in urban areas is 60kph (36mph) while on the open road it is 120kph (72mph). Limits are strictly enforced and the police often set up radar speed traps, so do not be tempted to exceed the limit as the fines are high.

**Car Hire:** There are a range of car-hire companies:

*Francistown:* **Avis**, tel: 241 3901, e-mail: avisfwn@botsnet.bw **Budget**, tel: 244 0083, fax: 241 8292; **Destiny**, tel: 241 8787, fax: 241 8772; **Imperial**, tel: 240 4281.

*Gaborone:* **Avis**, tel: 391 3093, e-mail: botswanares@avis.co.bw **Budget**, tel: 390 2030, fax: 390 2028; **Select**, tel: 397 1240, e-mail: info@selectcarhire.co.bw **Imperial**, tel: 390 7233, fax: 390 9404.

*Kasane:* **Avis**, tel: 625 0144, fax: 625 0145.

*Maun:* **Avis**, tel: 686 0039, e-mail: avismun@botsnet.bw **Budget**, tel: 686 3728, fax: 686 3563.

**Petrol and Diesel:** Petrol stations can be found along major highways around Botswana and fuel is available 24 hours a day in the main centres. Diesel and unleaded petrol are available in Botswana.

**Maps:** Maps of Botswana are scarce, but a good map highlighting the national parks is available from the Department of Tourism (P/Bag 0047, Gaborone, tel: 395 3024) and international embassies, trade missions and Air Botswana offices. Shell Oil Botswana has produced excellent maps by Veronica Roodt, while the Globetrotter maps of Botswana are recommended and are available at larger reputable bookshops in most major cities. Detailed maps are also available from the Department of Surveys and Mapping in Gaborone, tel: 395 3251.

## What to Pack

The dress code is casual in Botswana, particularly on safari, and even in the centres of Gaborone and Francistown few restaurants insist on a standard of dress. But do not wear camouflaged or military-style clothing as this, as well as topless or nude swimming is against the law in Botswana.

**Note:** internal flights within Botswana particularly to the camps in the Delta, Chobe and Tuli areas are generally in single or twin engine aircraft which have a strict **10kg baggage allowance**. If the flight is full any excess baggage will be left behind. Take only the essentials, i.e. lightweight summer clothing in neutral shades, long trousers and a long-sleeved shirt, track suit, warm jacket, comfortable walking shoes, hat, swimming costume, sunglasses, thick socks, sunscreen, malaria tablets, insect repellent and a torch.

A camera and bird-watching binoculars are also important. These should be packed into soft carry bags to ensure that they fit into the hold of smaller charter aircraft.

## Money Matters

The currency in Botswana (Pula) is strong and easily exchangeable. It is divided into 100 thebe. Notes are in denominations of P200, P100, P50, P20 and P10. Coins are in denominations of P5, P2, P1, 50t, 25t, 10t and 5t.

**Currency Exchange:** Money can be exchanged at banks, hotels and bureaus de change.

**Banks:** Generally most banks are open from 09:00–15:30. Some banks close early on Wednesday and they are all closed by 11:30 on Saturdays.

**Credit Cards:** Visa, Mastercard and American Express are accepted by a variety of outlets and most hotels, lodges and safari operators will accept recognizable foreign currency and travellers' cheques.

**Tipping:** It is important to tip your mokoro poler, safari camp assistants, game ranger

## CONVERSION CHART

| From | To | Multiply By |
|------|------|-------------|
| Millimetres | Inches | 0.0394 |
| Metres | Yards | 1.0936 |
| Metres | Feet | 3.281 |
| Kilometres | Miles | 0.6214 |
| Square kilometres | Square miles | 0.386 |
| Hectares | Acres | 2.471 |
| Litres | Pints | 1.760 |
| Kilograms | Pounds | 2.205 |
| Tonnes | Tons | 0.984 |
| To convert Celsius to Fahrenheit: x 9 ÷ 5 + 32 | | |

and guide and this can be done either at the time or as an extra when paying your bill at the end of your stay. While not mandatory, tipping is also expected in restaurants.

## Accommodation
A star grading system has been introduced in Botswana and, while the cost is usually a good indication of quality, many accommodation establishments and their star grading can be found in a directory on the Botswana Tourism website at www.botswanatourism.co.bw The largest international hotel group is **Cresta Marakanelo** (tel: 391 2222, fax: 390 4329, e-mail: reservations@cresta hotels.com), which operates a range of hotels in Botswana. Other hotel groups represented are **Peermont** with a selection of **Walmont** and **Mondior** hotels and the **South African Sun International** group who operates a leading hotel and casino in Gaborone.

There are numerous other **luxury lodges** and **safari camps** in Botswana's tourist areas which offer outstanding accommodation, cuisine and service. Accommodation in these safari camps is usually in large meru-style tents with *en suite* facilities.

There are a few **motels** in Botswana found in the towns along the major roads. **Self-catering** accommodation is available at some of the safari and rest camps, but facilities are rudimentary, generally being little more than a barbecue site. There are no youth hostels in Botswana,

**PUBLIC HOLIDAYS**

**1 & 2 January**
New Year
**4 days, usually in early April** • Easter
**1 May** • Labour Day
**Mid-May** • Ascension Day
**1 July** Sir Seretse Khama Day
**15 July** • President's Day
**30 September** • Botswana Day (Indepedence)
**25 December** Christmas Day
**26 December** • Boxing Day

save for a **YWCA** in Gaborone and, with the generally high cost of travel and low volumes of traffic, **backpacking** options are limited.

**Camping** is available at designated sites within the national parks and at privately owned sites throughout the country, but generally the facilities are limited. It is possible to camp in any public rural area, but be sure to ask permission from the local chief and be very careful to leave no litter or open fires behind. **Caravanning** is not an option in Botswana as most of the roads to the tourist areas are extremely rough and consequently there are no facilities for caravans even if you were able to get there.

## Trading Hours
Most shops in Botswana are open from 08:30–17:00 during the week, and from 09:00–13:00 on Saturdays. In the more remote areas shops still follow the traditional hours,

closing slightly later in the evening, but often shutting for lunch. Government offices are open from 07:30–16:30 and are closed for lunch from 12:30–13:45, Mon–Fri.

## Communications
**Telephone and Fax:** Botswana has one of the most sophisticated telecommunications systems in Africa. STD dialling is available to almost anywhere in the world (dial 00 to access the international satellite followed by the necessary codes). Public coin and card phones are available in most villages, while the remote camps are linked to their urban offices by radio. Phone cards are available at most large retail stores or post offices. Due to the sophistication of this network and the small number of users, telephone services in Botswana are expensive. Cellular phones are widely used throughout Botswana and there are two GSM cellular service providers; **Mascom**, tel: 390 3396 and **Orange**, tel: 316 3370. Both have roaming agreements with most countries and can provide temporary pre-paid numbers to visitors with their own handsets. The Botswana Telecommunications Corporation, tel: 395 8000, publishes a telephone directory for the country every year. Almost all hotels offer a fax and e-mail service to guests, and the larger establishments usually have full secretarial services available with e-mail and Internet access. There are Internet cafés in most of Botswana's urban centres.

**Postal Services:** Even the remotest of villages usually has a post office and the service in Botswana is cheap and reliable, if somewhat slow.

## Time

Botswana operates on Central African Time (CAT) – two hours ahead of Greenwich Mean (or Universal Standard) Time, one hour ahead of European Winter Time and seven hours ahead of the USA's Eastern Standard Time.

## Electricity

The power system in Botswana is 220V AC 50 Hz. Both round and square plugs are used so it is worth bringing adaptors for both. Lodges and camps in the tourist areas are generally not on the national power grid and rely on solar power or generators, which sometimes do not provide enough power for the use of hair dryers.

## Weights and Measures

Botswana uses the metric system.

## Medical Services

Pharmacies sell all necessary medicines and there are many of them including the Pharma group, tel: 318 2767 or 390 6688. Any pharmacy will be able to recommend a good local doctor if needed. **MRI Botswana,** tel: 390 3066, offers a medical rescue and evacuation service to members, and the **Gaborone Private Hospital**, tel: 368 5600, is a fully equipped top-quality medical institution. Most tour operators do not provide

clients with any insurance and visitors are recommended to arrange their own health and travel insurance before arriving, although it is well worth combining this with a local medical rescue cover.

## Health Hazards

**Malaria** is endemic in northern Botswana and visitors should take the full course of anti-malaria tablets, before, during and after their trip. Although it is possible, the chances of contracting bilharzia are remote. **AIDS** is widespread, so avoid casual unprotected sex. After the first rains (Oct–Dec) in livestock areas there is a resurgence of **tick bite fever**. Insect repellent, long trousers and socks are a good deterrent, but check for ticks after walking through long grass. Tetracycline pills are effective in curing tick bite fever, but the full course must be taken. Hepatitis A has been recorded in Botswana. While infection is unlikely visitors can have Gamma globulin injections prior to arrival which offer six months protection against the disease.

## Emergencies

In case of emergency dial 997 for an ambulance, 998 for the fire brigade, 999 for the police, and for MRI Medical Rescue members 911.

## Security

Apart from licensed hunting rifles, guns are not available to the general public. Although there is the occasional armed robbery and with the close proximity of the South African

border to Gaborone, cars are sometimes stolen in the city, there is generally very little violent crime. Visitors should be aware of petty theft and pickpocketing and take sensible precautions, keeping cash and valuables locked away or out of sight. Bribery is frowned upon and the Directorate on Corruption and Economic Crime actively prosecutes anyone offering or accepting a bribe, so do not consider it. It is a male-dominated society in Botswana, so foreign women should be prepared for some conservative traditional attitudes, and unaccompanied women may also attract a degree of attention, particularly in the frontier towns. While the streets are generally safe in Botswana it is still worth using common sense.

## Good Reading

- A good bird reference book such as **Roberts' Birds of Southern Africa**, Gordon Lindsay, or **Newman's Birds of Southern Africa** and **Sasol Birds of Southern Africa**, Kenneth Newman.
- **Mammals of Botswana** (a field guide), Peter Comley and Salome Meyer,
- **Land Mammals of southern Africa**, Reay Smithers.
- **Signs of the Wild**, Clive Walker.
- **Trees of the Okavango Delta and Moremi Game Reserve,** Veronica Roodt.
- **Kalahari. Life's variety in dune and delta**, Michael Main.

# INDEX

# *Beautiful*
# BIRDS
## *of*
# SEYCHELLES

**Adrian Skerrett**

*Camerapix Publishers International*
### NAIROBI

This edition published 1997 by
Camerapix Publishers International Limited
PO Box 45048
Nairobi
Kenya

First impression 1994

Second impression 1997

© Camerapix 1994

ISBN 1-874041-70-9

This book was designed and produced by
Camerapix Publishers International Limited

Printed in Hong Kong by South China Printing Co (1988) Ltd.

*Page 1: Lesser noddy gather on a tree roost on Bird Island.*
*Previous pages: The graceful fairy tern with their blue bills, are now commonly
found on both Cousin and Aride Island.*
*Opposite: Bird watchers on Aride's towering cliffs enjoy an avian spectacular.*
*Following pages: More than a million sooty terns make their home on Bird Island.*

# Contents

*Above: Moorhens with their brightly-coloured frontal headshields and bills are becoming a rare sight, but can be found close to pools and marshes on most of the granitic islands.*

# Preface

This book covers nearly all the breeding bird species of Seychelles, together with some of the more common migrants likely to be seen. As island nations tend to have fewer species than continental ones, a book of this size is able to be fairly comprehensive, providing description and interesting facts about the birds of Seychelles as well as information on their distribution. However, it is not possible to cover all of the 200 or so species found on the islands, many of which have been recorded only a few times. The keen ornithologist will need to seek other references to track down these rarities.

Nevertheless, for the visitor who wants to know what the red bird is that he saw in the hotel gardens, or the noisy starling-like bird in the trees, or the little character with a curved bill a bit like a hummingbird, here are the answers. Likewise for those interested in the special outer islands — especially Aldabra — there is a section which will hopefully whet the appetite for a visit further afield one day. Where a species occurs in both the granitic islands and the outer isles, it has been illustrated in the former section only, with its distribution noted in the text.

Keep your eyes peeled in Seychelles — during the migratory seasons you can expect the unexpected. Many new species have been recorded by visiting bird groups and other tourists. There is no official bird list as yet, although a Records Committee has been formed. Any interesting records would be welcomed by Mr Adrian Skerrett, Secretary, Seychelles Bird Records Committee, c/o Mahé Shipping Co. Ltd., P.O. Box 336, Victoria, Mahé Seychelles.

# Introduction

Tropical island birds have a special fascination and beauty. Their homes have been transformed by time into worlds within a world. The ocean acts as a barrier to prevent outsiders from breaking into this world, and within its fortress nature evolves new and fascinating forms.

Seychelles is rich in birds found nowhere else, either as unique species or sub-species: nature's stepping stones between a continental variety and the emergence of a new form. The total number of species is not great. It is possible to see more species in East Africa in a single day than could be seen in Seychelles in a lifetime. However, it includes some of the rarest and most endangered birds on earth and there is a special thrill for the expert and beginner alike to know that what he is seeing can be found nowhere else on the planet.

Apart from the land birds which managed to cross to Seychelles, the islands have inevitably been colonized by ocean wanderers: birds such as the Sooty Tern and the Wedge-tailed Shearwater which eat and sleep at sea, and return to land only to breed. Seychelles has some of the most spectacular seabird colonies to be found anywhere. Aride Island is rightly known as the Seabird Citadel of the Indian Ocean, with ten breeding species, and the nearby reserve of Cousin boasts seven species. The noise and density of birds at the height of the breeding season is incredible, evoking images of Alfred Hitchcock's thriller *The Birds* and reminding one to whom these islands really belong.

A world apart is Aldabra, a World Heritage Site, where the last remaining flightless bird of the Indian Ocean islands still survives. Here, primitive frigatebirds and comical boobies nest in dense colonies, while a host of Aldabran specialities abound ashore. Few sunseekers drawn to Seychelles shores will have the opportunity to visit remote, wild, unspoilt Aldabra, but even those who cannot visit will be interested to learn of that

Seychelles island just over the horizon where nature has gone wild in its own special way.

The world's only ocean islands of granite — a fragment of the ancient supercontinent of Gondwanaland — have specialities which add to the pleasure of discovering each new island. Even Mahé — home to ninety per cent of Seychellois and by far the most developed island — has two species found here and nowhere else in the world. The Black Parrot is the symbol of Praslin, while the inhabitants of La Digue are justly proud of the Seychelles Paradise Flycatcher. Cousin is famous for the Seychelles Warbler, now successfully introduced to Aride and Cousine, while no visitor to Frégate can fail to be aware it is home to Seychelles' rarest bird, the Seychelles Magpie-robin.

Island populations are especially vulnerable to the ravages of man, but Seychelles has fared much better than other island nations of the Indian Ocean. Just one full species has been definitely lost — the Green Parakeet — shot because of its liking for fruit planted by early settlers. However, the Aldabran Brush Warbler, only discovered in 1967, has not been seen since 1983 and may now also be extinct. One subspecies, the Chestnut Flanked White-eye, recorded only on Marianne, has also been lost, and other subspecies may have disappeared even before they had been recorded by science.

Nevertheless, much remains, and nature is now making a comeback. Scientific research on Aride, Cousin, Frégate and Aldabra is helping to unlock the secrets that will help us understand what is needed to reverse the process of destruction. There are already signs of success, such as the spread of Seychelles Warblers on Aride, though much remains to be done.

Meanwhile, the birds of Seychelles live out their lives to the rhythm of the seasons. Not summer or winter here, just south

of the Equator, but the varying conditions on land and at sea brought about by the changing monsoon winds.

The south-east monsoon brings drier, less humid conditions from May to September. It also brings plankton-rich waters from further south and an abundance of fish. This is the time for the great tern colonies to breed. The Sooty Tern on Bird, Aride and Desnoeufs, the Lesser Noddy on Aride and Cousin and rarities such as the Roseate Tern, now only known to breed on Aride in the granitic islands — all are drawn from their ocean realm to the noise and excitement of the tightly packed breeding colonies.

October may bring the first rains of the north-west monsoon, which signal the appearance of an abundance of food for land birds to start to breed. Some species of both land and seabird may breed at any time of year, while the onset of the northern winter is the time rare vagrants from northern climes may turn up. At this time of year, the possibility that almost any Eurasian migrant could fly in makes for exciting birdwatching.

Even the introduced birds, such as the brilliant scarlet Madagascar Fody, or the more elusive Waxbill, have their interest in their adopted home. Like the people of Seychelles, the birds have a mixture of origins, drawn from different corners of the globe and integrated into a unique and fascinating avifauna.

# 1. BIRDS OF THE GRANITIC ISLANDS

**GREEN-BACKED HERON** (Makak, Manik)
*Butorides striatus*

Two subspecies of this small heron occur in Seychelles: *crawfordi* in the Amirantes and at Aldabra, which is believed to be of Asian origin, and *degens* in the granitic islands, which curiously may be closer to the African race. If correct, the reason for this strange overlap is unknown and is a reminder of how Seychelles' avifauna has its origins where these two continents parted company.

The Green-backed Heron feeds along the shore, in mangroves and in inland marshy areas, where it is sometimes confused with the Chinese Bittern. It is usually seen hunched and solitary, waiting motionless for fish, crabs and occasionally lizards and insects to pass within range. Sometimes it moves as if in slow motion to sneak up on prey.

The bird is generally greyish-brown with bright orange feet, visible when it flies away. When taking off, it frequently makes a harsh croak — 'makak' — giving the bird its Creole name.

The nest is usually solitary, about thirty centimetres (one foot) across. Two or three pale blue eggs are laid in the shallow bowl of the nest. It may nest at any time of year, but more usually during the north-west monsoon.

*Illustrated on following page*

## CATTLE EGRET (Madanm Paton)
*Bubulcus ibis seychellarum*

This elegant, slender heron-like bird is found throughout Seychelles. The name originates from its habit of following cattle in order to snap up flies and other insects. It is a common sight in Victoria Market and around rubbish dumps, where it replaces the gulls, crows and other scavengers not commonly found in Seychelles.

The pure white bird develops golden cinnamon feathers on its breast and head when breeding. Its legs change from black to purple and its bill from yellow to pink.

Cattle Egrets nest and roost in colonies, one of the largest being at Le Chantier on the southern edge of Victoria.

This Seychelles subspecies needs further study but it is believed to be of Asian origin as it is smaller than average, like the Asian form.

*Illustrated on previous page*

## GREY HERON (Florentin)
*Ardea cinerea*

The large Grey Heron is found throughout Seychelles. Although it breeds in small numbers in the granitic islands, it is far more common in the Amirantes, Farquhar and the Aldabra group.

The only large heron recorded in Seychelles, it is usually seen in open coastal reef flats, lagoon shorelines or on Mahé, along the mudflats next to the reclaimed land around Victoria.

The Grey Heron is a tall, grey-backed bird with a black strip along the side of the head, which is otherwise white. Adults have black head plumes. The legs and bill are grey but may turn pinkish-red during breeding.

An untidy nest of twigs is built in mangroves or low cover. Occasionally it may nest on the ground. Two to four pale blue eggs are laid.

The diet includes fish, crabs, baby turtles and the chicks of some birds, such as Sooty Terns, in the Amirantes.

*Illustrated on following page*

## SEYCHELLES KESTREL (Katiti)
*Falco araea*

The only bird of prey breeding in the granitic islands, there are some 200 pairs of Seychelles Kestrel on Mahé and about ten on Praslin, where it was introduced in 1977. Up to forty pairs survive on Silhouette, and a few pairs on La Digue.

The Seychelles Kestrel is much smaller than its European counterpart. It has chestnut wings with black spots, a dark crown and unmarked underparts. It nests in church towers or taller buildings, as well as on mountain rock ledges.

Usually heard before it is seen, the Creole name is said to resemble its harsh cry. They eat lizards, large insects, rats and mice. An old Creole name of *Manze Poul*, or 'Chicken Eater', gave the kestrel an undeserved reputation as a bird of ill omen and a harbinger of death. Many were killed due to such superstitions but this is now largely a thing of the past.

*Illustrated on previous page*

## MOORHEN (Pouldo)
*Gallinula chloropus*

Identical to the European race, though possibly a little smaller, some consider this moorhen to be a separate subspecies, *seychellarum*. It is fairly common close to pools and marshes on all the main granitic islands; but is most commonly seen on Aride and Cousin and in the pools by the Plantation Club on Mahé.

Both sexes are black with a red frontal shield and white undertail feathers. It may eat small fish, insects, lizards and vegetation.

Breeding takes place year-round; each pair establishing a territory. About six eggs are laid, though usually only one or two chicks survive. The moorhen is becoming a rare sight as marshes are drained to make way for houses and agriculture.

Though a reluctant flier, and a bird which skulks through the undergrowth, this remarkably successful species is found throughout the world except for the Australasian region.

*Illustrated on following page*

## BARRED GROUND DOVE (Tourtrel koko)
*Geopelia striata*

Also known as Barred Dove, Zebra Dove and Peaceful Dove, this charming little bird has been introduced from its native South-east Asia to islands from St. Helena to Hawaii. In Seychelles it has probably been introduced from Malaysia via Mauritius and is now one of the most common birds of the granitic islands.

The Barred Ground Dove is the only small dove found in Seychelles. It is light pinkish-brown below, barred with black on the flanks, and has brownish upperparts. The long narrow tail is raised and spread in the courtship display, revealing white outer feathers.

It may breed year-round, but more usually during the north-west monsoon. The nest is usually high in trees where two white eggs are laid.

The Barred Ground Dove is a seed eater, but is commonly seen around houses and hotels where it can become very tame. The high-pitched coo is one of the most common bird sounds heard around Seychelles wherever there is human settlement.

*Illustrated on previous page*

## MALAGASY TURTLE DOVE (Tourtrel dezil)
*Streptopelia picturata*

Turtle doves of Malagasy origin have developed into at least three different subspecies in Seychelles: *rostrata* in the granitic islands, *aldabrana* (a misnomer) in the Amirantes, and *coppingeri* on Aldabra.

The granitic islands' variety has now almost disappeared due to breeding with the slightly larger introduced Malagasy form. The former has a reddish-brown head, while the latter has a grey head. Only on Cousin and Cousine are red-headed forms frequently seen, and even there the pure Seychelles race probably no longer exists.

The Malagasy Turtle Dove is a fruit eater, eating wild figs and seeds, but also introduced fruits such as paw paws and bananas. It will also take insects.

Breeding takes place mainly during the north-west monsoon when the rains make food more plentiful. Two white eggs are laid in an untidy twig nest.

*Illustrated on following page*

## SEYCHELLES BLUE PIGEON (Pizon Olande)
*Alectroenas pulcherrima*

Unique to Seychelles, and fairly common on Mahé, Praslin, La Digue and especially Frégate, this is one of the most attractive birds of the islands.

It has a scarlet wattle on the crown and forehead, a white bib and an indigo-blue body. This colour scheme earned it its Creole name, which refers to the Dutch flag.

The Seychelles Blue Pigeon can be seen in forests from sea-level upwards, but is most common in the mountains. It will eat almost any fruit. Its muscular gizzard is capable of breaking up and digesting seeds so that it does not spread its food plants in the manner of other pigeons, and depends much more on habitat conservation than other birds. On the other hand, it adapts well to introduced fruits such as guava and cinnamon berries.

The female alone builds the platform nest, where one or two eggs will be laid. During the breeding season the birds engage in impressive display flights, flying high above the trees, then swooping down steeply.

The bird is often heard before it is seen: there is no mistaking the pigeon-like coo.

*Illustrated on previous page*

## BLACK PARROT (Kato nwar)
*Coracopsis nigra barklyi*

Oddly enough, with a wealth of unique species, Seychelles has chosen as its national bird this subspecies of the Lesser Vasa Parrot of Madagascar. However, the Black Parrot is the only remaining parrot in Seychelles following the extinction of the native Green Parakeet and introduced Grey-headed Lovebird. It is a remarkable bird found in the equally remarkable Vallée de Mai.

It is dark brown in colour with a heavy, typical parrot's bill and black legs. At rest it is unmistakably a parrot, but in flight it can be confused with the Blue Pigeon — which has more pointed wings and a prominent head, in contrast to the hunched appearance of the Black Parrot.

A high-pitched whistle is usually the first sign of a parrot's presence. The dense vegetation of the Vallée de Mai can make the Black Parrot difficult to locate, but it may also be seen around the periphery and in the lowlands. Recently, the parrot has invaded Curieuse.

Up to three eggs are laid, usually in holes of dead trees. Breeding takes place during the north-west monsoon, but parents may still be feeding fledged young in June or July.

The diet is fruit and flowers, including introduced species such as guava, mango and bilimbi.

*Illustrated on following page*

## SEYCHELLES BARE-LEGGED SCOPS OWL (Syer)
*Otus insularis*

The only owl found naturally in Seychelles may be related to the Moluccan Scops Owl, which has a similar call and is also similar in size and plumage. If they are related, this is the first and only evidence of a link between the avifauna of the western Indian Ocean and Australasia.

The Seychelles Bare-legged Scops Owl is confined to the mountains of Mahé, where up to eighty pairs may survive. More often heard than seen, its rasping cry gives the bird its Creole name meaning 'woodcutter'.

It is a small, dark brown owl with bare legs and small ear tufts. Thought to be extinct from 1906 to 1959, its rediscovery by local ornithologist Phillipe Loustau-Lalanne caused a sensation. It was probably always known to people living in the hills, and indeed a skin of a bird collected in 1940 came to light after its rediscovery.

No nest has ever been discovered and much about the bird remains a mystery. Its diet is thought to be lizards and large insects, and it probably nests among boulders and on cliff ledges.

*Illustrated on previous page*

## BARN OWL (Ibou)
*Tyto alba*

It is a little ironic that the Barn Owl is endangered and protected throughout much of its range, while in Seychelles it is considered a pest with a bounty on its head. Introduced in 1951 and 1952 to control rats, it is said to have done considerable damage to the endemic fauna and seabird colonies.

As the only large owl with pale spotted underparts and a circular white face, it is quite unmistakable. It can often be seen at night, caught in the headlights of a car, or patrolling a rubbish dump on the lookout for rats or mice.

The Fairy Tern is the Barn Owl's favoured prey on the seabird islands, where its pure white plumage gives away its presence in the dark. Other birds and lizards will also be taken.

Nests are built among rocks, in church towers or in trees. From six to eight whitish eggs are usually laid. Like most owls, the eggs hatch in the order in which they are laid so that there will be young of different ages within the same nest.

The Barn Owl was once reported to be common on Aldabra, but it has now vanished for unknown reasons.

*Illustrated on following page*

## SEYCHELLES CAVE SWIFTLET (Irondel)
*Aerodramus elaphrus*

The Seychelles Cave Swiftlet — the only swallow-like bird breeding in Seychelles — is of a genus whose fourteen other representatives are found entirely in Asia and Australasia, except for the Mascarene Swiftlet. It is fairly common on the main granitic islands, although no nest was found until 1970.

The swiftlet nests in caves where it uses an echo-locating metallic call in the darkness. The bracket-shaped nest is made of lichens held together with saliva, similar to the closely related Edible-nest Swiftlet of South-east Asia. Unlike most of the Seychelles land birds, it nests at the beginning of the south-east monsoon.

The Seychelles Cave Swiftlet is a dark bird, grey-brown above and a little paler below. Its diet consists of flying insects taken on the wing.

*Illustrated on previous page*

## SEYCHELLES BULBUL (Merl)
*Hypsipetes crassirostris*

In the hills, the noisy, inquisitive Seychelles Bulbul is one of the most common birds to be seen. It draws attention to its presence through a variety of hoarse calls and shrieks as it flits from tree to tree and chases other bulbuls through the forest. It also imitates the calls of other birds — including the mynah, who itself is a mimic.

Dark olive to grey-brown with a shaggy — but not very noticeable — crest, the adult Seychelles Bulbul has a bright orange bill. It cannot be mistaken for any other Seychelles bird, except perhaps on Praslin, from a distance, for the Black Parrot. However, the build of the bulbul is more streamlined than the typical plump, large-headed parrot.

Its diet is mainly insects and berries, including those of introduced plants such as lantana. It is of a genus of Asian origin with a stronger flight and greater liking for dense undergrowth than other bulbuls.

A cup-shaped nest is built, usually in the fork of a tree, at the beginning of the north-west monsoon. Two bright pink eggs, speckled with brown, are laid.

*Illustrated on following page*

## SEYCHELLES MAGPIE-ROBIN (Pi Santez)
*Copsychus sechellarum*

This is the rarest of the unique birds of the granitic islands of Seychelles. Once widespread throughout the area, it was wiped out by rats, cats, competition with introduced birds, loss of habitat and the one-time practice of keeping them as cage birds. Today, almost all the forty or so Seychelles Magpie-robins are confined to Frégate Island.

It is an unmistakable black-and-white bird of the thrush family. The genus is widespread in Asia, though the Seychelles form is probably most closely related to the Malagasy species. It is unusually large and dark for a magpie-robin, and the ginger coloration present in nearly all others of this family appears only in the wing patches of the immature Seychelles version.

An untidy round nest is built in the tops of trees, especially palms, in which one pale blue egg is laid. Breeding takes place mainly during the north-west monsoon when the rains increase the availability of insects and other food.

A recovery programme is being implemented. Aride Island was selected as the most suitable island for a second population and the first transfer took place in 1992.

*Illustrated on previous page*

## SEYCHELLES WARBLER (Timerl dezil)
*Acrocephalus sechellensis*

By 1959, just twenty-six Seychelles Warblers were left on earth, all of them on tiny Cousin Island. The bird had been wiped out from Marianne and possibly other islands due to habitat destruction. Cousin was purchased in 1968 principally to save it from extinction.

Following the regeneration of the original forest, its numbers increased dramatically. Able to establish and survive in small territories better than practically any other passerine — and with non-breeding birds assisting closely related breeding birds — the population reached almost 400 by 1987.

Twenty-nine birds were introduced to Aride in 1988 and a substantial population now flourishes there. A further successful introduction was made to Cousine in 1990, and this tiny insectivorous warbler has now been removed from the Red Data list of endangered birds.

Seychelles Warblers will breed at any time of year, given sufficient food availability. Cooperative breeding, usually involving adult offspring of the nesting pair, is practised where habitat is limited. Helpers generally enjoy greater success when they eventually establish their own territory. On Aride and Cousine — where the birds have been introduced — this habit was abandoned due to the plentiful habitat.

*Illustrated on following page*

## SEYCHELLES PARADISE FLYCATCHER (Vev)
*Terpsiphone corvina*

The beautiful Seychelles Paradise Flycatcher is the symbol of La Digue. Apart from a few birds on neighbouring Praslin, almost all the world's population of about seventy-five individuals are found there; mainly in the western coastal plateau in surviving stands of *Takamaka* and Indian Almond woodland.

The all-black plumage of the male bird gives it the local name, meaning 'widow'. In bright sunlight, it has a deep blue sheen, but it is the long tail streamers which make it quite unmistakable. The female is chestnut above and white below, with a black face and crown.

Breeding takes place during the north-west monsoon, when a cup-shaped nest is built near the end of a branch. Usually just one egg is laid. Chicks are reared by both males and females. The juvenile resembles the female until its first moult, but is duller in colour.

A reserve at La Passe on La Digue has been created to help protect the bird, which once had a much wider distribution. First reported from Praslin, it also once occurred on Marianne, Félicité and probably other islands in the area.

*Illustrated on previous page*

## SEYCHELLES SUNBIRD (Kolibri)
*Nectarinia dussumieri*

The most common of the granitic islands' unique birds, the Seychelles Sunbird is found from the coast to the higher hills on almost all the main islands. It is the only endemic bird commonly seen flitting around the trees in hotel grounds, in Victoria and most gardens.

It is dull compared with most sunbirds, but in breeding plumage the male has a deep metallic-blue throat and orange pectoral tufts, visible during display. The female is drab: dull brown above, lighter below.

Nesting takes place mainly during the north-west monsoon. A typical sunbird nest is built, oval in shape with a porch leading to the nesting chamber. Constructed from grass, Casuarina needles, spiders' webs and scraps of string or other debris, the interior is lined with feathers and kapok. The female builds the nest and lays a single egg.

The diet is mainly nectar, and the bird's success is largely due to its successful adaptation to garden plants including hibiscus, cordia and other flowers.

*Illustrated on following page*

47

## SEYCHELLES WHITE-EYE (Zwazo bannann)
*Zosterops modesta*

Thought to be extinct from 1936 until it was rediscovered in 1962, the Seychelles White-eye remains one of the rarest and most endangered of Seychelles birds. It is confined to Mahé, where a small number of individuals survive between 300 and 600 metres (1,000 to 2,000 feet) in the northern half of the island.

It is a small grey-brown bird with pale underparts. At close range or with binoculars, a white ring round the eye readily distinguishes it from any other bird. Often it will be heard before it is seen; its soft, sporadic calls are quite unlike the harsher calls of the sunbirds and fodies, which may be seen in the same areas.

Both members of a pair help to build a small cup-shaped nest. It breeds at both the beginning and end of the north-west monsoon, selecting a nest site in dense vegetation. Outside the breeding times, nomadic feeding parties may be seen. These separate into pairs for breeding, although non-breeding helpers may sometimes assist a breeding pair. Such cooperative breeding is rare in white-eyes, although it is a highly social bird. This behaviour has only been confirmed in the Mascarene Grey White-eye.

The scarcity of the bird is a little strange considering white-eyes are generally among the most common endemic passerines in other Indian Ocean countries. Also, it appears at home in secondary forest and feeds on insects in introduced trees such as cloves, breadfruit and albizia, which are found in areas with a lot of human activity. In the nineteenth century it was described as being 'tolerably abundant' and the reasons for its decline remain unclear.

*Illustrated on previous page*

## INDIAN MYNAH (Marten)
*Acridotheres tristis*

The most common and most obvious land bird of Seychelles, the mynah was introduced from India via Mauritius around 1830, possibly as a cage bird, or — as was the case in Mauritius — to control locusts.

Dark brown with white wing patches, this noisy, gregarious bird also has a yellow bill, legs and facial skin. Sometimes a mutant form with a bald yellow head and neck can be seen, especially on Mahé; this is known locally as a King Mynah, and legend attributes its features to over-indulgence in ripe mangoes.

Two or three small, blue eggs are laid in an untidy nest built in trees or buildings. It will eat almost anything — including carrion — and can even be seen hunting for food on the seashore.

*Illustrated on following page*

## MADAGASCAR FODY (Kardinal)
*Foudia madagascariensis*

This species is now the most common land bird of the granitic Seychelles. A naturalist visiting Seychelles in 1866 found only one fody on Mahé, and it was probably introduced as a cage bird around this date. It also occurs throughout most of the Amirantes and on Farquhar.

The breeding male fody in his scarlet plumage is unmistakable from October to March. A few reddish males may be seen outside these dates, but during the south-east monsoon it loses its breeding dress and resembles the dull brown females.

A domed nest is woven, often high up in coconut palms, in which two — sometimes three — glossy, pale blue eggs are laid. Nest building is done mainly by the male.

Other local names are *sren* and, on La Digue, *taroza*.

*Illustrated on previous page*

## SEYCHELLES FODY (Tok tok)
*Foudia sechellarum*

This bird survives on the rat-free islands of Cousin, Cousine and Frégate, where there are perhaps a total of 4,000 birds. The Seychelles Fody formerly occurred on Marianne and La Digue, and possibly also on Praslin and Aride.

There is little difference between the sexes, although the male sports a yellow facial patch in breeding plumage. Otherwise it is a rather dull, dark, sparrow-like bird.

It is aggressive, and is a superior hunter to the Madagascar Fody. The diet is mainly insects with some fruit and seeds and a small amount of nectar. It usually nests in bushy trees, and lays just one egg — whereas the Madagascar Fody nests almost exclusively in coconut palms and will usually lay two eggs.

The two species appear to co-exist quite happily, probably because of the adaptive features of an insectivorous and a seed-eating species, and divergent adaptation to different environments of origin — the *tok tok* to the forests of Seychelles and the *kardinal* to the more open countryside of Madagascar.

*Illustrated on following page*

# 2. BIRDS OF THE OUTER ISLANDS

**DIMORPHIC EGRET** (Zegret blan ek nwar)
*Egretta dimorpha*

Also known as Madagascar Egret, this species, found only in Madagascar and the Aldabra group, was until recently classed as a subspecies of the Little Egret, but some authorities claim to be sufficiently distinct to be regarded separately. Occasional vagrants turn up in the Amirantes and the granitic islands.

Taller and more slender than the Cattle Egret, it has a black bill and legs with bright yellow or orange feet. There is yellow facial skin around the bill and long plumes hang from the back of the crown.

Oddly, adult birds may be pure white or jet black, with very occasional pied forms. White birds are more common, although at least one-quarter of the population is black.

The diet is mainly small fish and crustaceans, which it stalks in rock pools and shallow waters — often feeding in pairs or small groups.

It breeds during the north-west monsoon, building a large platform nest in which two or three light blue eggs are laid. Chicks stay with their parents, learning the art of hunting for several weeks after they leave the nest.

*Illustrated on previous page*

## ALDABRA SACRED IBIS (Ibis)
*Threskiornis aethiopica abbotti*

Widespread throughout Africa, this bird has evolved into a separate subspecies in Aldabra, which breeds only there and has never been recorded anywhere else. The total population is perhaps 1,000 birds.

The Aldabra Sacred Ibis is a large, white bird with a black, bald neck, black legs and black plumes, and a large, heavy, curved bill. Its eyes are china blue and its wings have very short black tips (compared with the red-brown eyes and noticeable black wing tips of its African relative). The juvenile has dark brown plumes and its neck is covered in white feathers at first, becoming bald within about one year; its eyes are brown, changing to white, then blue.

It occurs on the lagoon shore and around inland pools, where it probes in the mud for crabs and molluscs. Insects — and occasionally dead turtles and tortoises — may also be taken.

It breeds during the north-west monsoon in shrubs near water, building an untidy nest in which usually two large white eggs are laid. At one time it was far less common as, due to its tameness, it was hunted for food.

*Illustrated on following page*

## MALAGASY KESTREL (Katiti Aldabra)
*Falco newtoni*

Found only on Aldabra, the Malagasy Kestrel is probably a very recent arrival to Seychelles, as it is not significantly different from that which is found in Madagascar (although slightly smaller). Also, despite the lack of competition, it remains quite rare and is possibly still in the process of establishing itself.

It is probably related in some way to the Seychelles Kestrel and to the even rarer Mauritius Kestrel, but the relationship between the three species is not clearly understood. The Malagasy Kestrel differs from its granitic island cousin in having a streaked chest. It is bright chestnut above with black markings on the wings and a black streaked crown.

This kestrel is more abundant in open palm groves than in dense scrub, where it employs a perch-and-pounce policy to catch lizards and other prey.

Breeding takes place at the end of the dry south-east monsoon so that young are reared during the early months of the wet season when food is more plentiful.

*Illustrated on previous page*

## COMORO BLUE PIGEON (Pizon Olande Aldabra)
*Alectroenas sganzini minor*

This unique subspecies is found only on Aldabra, though a Blue Pigeon — possibly this one — was once reported to be common in Providence and Farquhar.

The head and neck are white with a silvery sheen; the rest of the body, wings, and tail are deep blue. The eye is surrounded by a conspicuous patch of red skin. The voice is a deep, hoarse 'coo' repeated several times.

The diet is fruits of native trees, and the population and distribution on Aldabra is limited mainly by the availability of this vegetation. It is more common at the eastern end of the atoll.

Breeding takes place during the north-west monsoon. A platform nest is built in which a single white egg is laid. Like the species of the granitic islands, it has a display flight in which it climbs steeply then swoops downward with wings held rigidly forward.

*Illustrated on following page*

## MALAGASY COUCAL (Toulouz)
*Centropus toulou insularis*

A large skulking bird, the Malagasy Coucal has a unique subspecies on Aldabra. The subspecies *assumptionis* from Assumption, now extinct, was probably identical to the Aldabran form.

When breeding during the north-west monsoon, the adult has glossy, jet-black plumage, except for the chestnut-coloured wings. The tail is long and heavy. Outside the breeding season, the black feathers change to streaky brown and the bill from black to brown.

A long tubular nest is built in bushes or low palm trees, in which up to four eggs are laid. Like many of the Aldabran land birds, it is more common at the eastern end of the atoll where there has been very little human disturbance.

The diet consists of lizards, insects and possibly the eggs and chicks of other birds. Often it is heard rather than seen, emitting a descending laughing call.

*Illustrated on previous page*

## MALAGASY BULBUL (Merl Aldabra)
*Hypsipetes madagascariensis rostratus*

This bulbul is fairly common on all the main islands of Aldabra Atoll, but is found nowhere else in the Aldabra group of islands. Small groups chase each other through the trees, constantly shrieking and calling to each other.

It is a fairly small bulbul, greyish-brown with a scruffy black crest, and a bright orange bill in the adult, which is dark brown when immature.

This subspecies of the Malagasy race, unique to Aldabra, has a wide diet including berries, fruits, flowers and insects.

Breeding commences early in the north-west monsoon. A cup-shaped nest is built in which usually two eggs are laid.

## RED-WHISKERED BULBUL
*Pycnonotus jocosus*

Introduced to Mauritius from South-east Asia in 1892, this bulbul is now one of the most common birds there. In 1976 and 1977, in contravention of Seychelles law, the Mauritian manager of Assumption introduced several alien land birds, this among them. Today the Red-whiskered Bulbul is widespread throughout the island, numbering perhaps 200 pairs.

It has a long upright black crest, white cheeks and red 'whiskers' below the eye. Immature birds lack the red patch on the cheek. The diet includes fruit, berries, seeds, flowers, nectar and insects. A cup-shaped nest is made in trees or bushes in which up to four eggs are laid.

*Illustrated on following page*

## SOUIMANGA SUNBIRD (Kolibri aldabra)
*Nectarinia sovimanga*

Originating from Madagascar, this sunbird has reached all the main islands of the Aldabra group, where it has evolved into three separate subspecies: *buchenorum* on Cosmoledo and Astove, *abbotti* on Assumption and *aldabrensis* on Aldabra.

The male has a red chest band and a metallic-green head. Yellow pectoral tufts are sometimes visible in the 'armpits'. The female is dark grey-brown above; light grey with brown streaks below. Both sexes have the typical decurved bill of sunbirds.

The diet includes both nectar and insects. Breeding takes place mainly during the north-west monsoon. A rugby-ball shaped nest is built, suspended from a thin branch, sometimes with a narrow 'porch' over it. Nest building is solely the responsibility of the female, who also does most of the feeding of the young. Up to three white eggs speckled with deep red are laid, though two eggs are more usual.

*Illustrated on previous page*

## MALAGASY WHITE-EYE (Sren aldabra)
*Zosterops maderaspatana aldabrensis*

Unlike the rare Seychelles White-eye, this is one of the most common birds of Aldabra, only a little less numerous than the Souimanga Sunbird. It can be seen all over Aldabra Atoll, including in mangroves where small parties of birds move through the trees. It is also present — but much less common — on Cosmoledo and Astove.

It is leaf green above, with a yellow forehead, chin and throat. It has a ring of white feathers around the eye, which is less obvious or absent in front of the eye.

Its cup-shaped nest is built in the fork of a tree or in a bush. Two pale bluish-green eggs are laid during the north-west monsoon. The diet includes insects, caterpillars, spiders, nectar and small fruits.

White-eyes are among the most successful island colonizers — probably because of their social behaviour, moving around in small groups. The Aldabran race originates from Madagascar, where the nominate form is the only white-eye species.

*Illustrated on following page*

*Above left: Aldabra Drongo (Juvenile)*
*Above right: Pied Crow*

## ALDABRA DRONGO (Moulanba)
*Dicrurus aldabranus*

Together with the Aldabra Brush Warbler, which may be extinct, this drongo is one of only two full species unique to Aldabra. Numbering perhaps 1,500 birds, it is distributed throughout the atoll, but is common nowhere.

The Aldabra Drongo is easily recognizable from its all-black plumage and deeply forked tail. It often sits in an open position on the lookout for insects and lizards.

Of Malagasy origin, it differs from other species in that the bill is unusually large. Juveniles are dark grey-brown above, paler below, whereas young birds of other species are black. The alarm call has been described as 'tit-po fo fa!', compared with the African Drongo's 'fa-fa tit-poo!'.

Two or three cream-coloured eggs with black and red specks at one end are laid in a cup-shaped nest. Breeding is at the beginning of the north-west monsoon.

## PIED CROW (Korbo)
*Corvus albus*

The only crow occurring naturally in Seychelles, this large black-and-white bird is fairly common on Aldabra and Astove. It also occurs on Cosmoledo and Assumption.

The Pied Crow breeds during the north-west monsoon, building nests high up in trees, especially palms and casuarinas. Up to six eggs are laid. The diet includes all kinds of invertebrates, eggs, seeds, fruits, corpses of tortoises and other carrion.

*Illustrated on previous page*

## WHITE-THROATED RAIL (Tyomityo)
*Dryolimnas cuvieri aldabranus*

This last remaining flightless bird of the Indian Ocean clings to existence only on Malabar and some of the smaller islands of Aldabra Atoll. The Dodo and Red Rail of Mauritius, the Solitaire and Legaut's Rail of Rodrigues, the White Dodo and Solitaire of Réunion, and the Elephant Bird of Madagascar were wiped out by man. Flightless Rails also disappeared from Astove and Assumption.

Olive-green above and chestnut below, with a white throat, the White-throated Rail is a tame, confiding bird which readily comes to investigate human presence. The bill is dark red at the base of the upper mandible in the male, and bright pink in the female.

It can run fast and uses its wings to scale rocks or other obstacles. It breeds during the north-west monsoon in a concealed fork of a bush or tree, laying three or four white eggs speckled with red.

Curiously, it may only be a subspecies of a rail occurring on Madagascar — which has retained the ability to fly.

It formerly occurred on all the main islands of the atoll and some large lagoon islets, but possibly was wiped out by feral cats on Picard and Grand Terre. It now only occurs on Malabar, Polymnie and Île Aux Cèdres, and probably on minor islets close to Malabar.

*Illustrated on following page*

*Above: Male*

*Left: Female*

## RED-HEADED FOREST FODY (Tisren aldabra)
*Foudia eminentissima aldabrana*

This unique subspecies is found all over Aldabra Atoll, and is similar to the Madagascar Fody and Seychelles Fody of the granitic islands. It is one of the most common land birds of the atoll.

During the breeding season, the male has a scarlet head and breast, yellow belly, and red rump. The female and non-breeding birds are dull, yellowish brown and streaky, resembling sparrows. All birds have heavy triangular bills.

Breeding takes place during the north-west monsoon. A spherical nest is built, mainly by the male, while the female incubates the two or three pale blue eggs. The diet is largely insects, but seeds and fruits will also be taken.

The species *eminentissima* has evolved either in Madagascar or the Comoros, and Aldabra has been colonized by one or other of these sources. The genus may be of earlier African origin.

*Illustrated on previous page*

# 3. THE SEABIRDS

## WEDGE-TAILED SHEARWATER (Fouke)
*Puffinus pacificus*

The only all dark-coloured shearwater breeding in the region, this species will frequently be seen on sea passages throughout Seychelles. It breeds in burrows on the few remaining rat-free islands, especially Aride and Cousin, with up to 20,000 and 10,000 pairs respectively. There are smaller colonies on Cousine, the Amirantes and a few small granitic islands.

Some burrows may be occupied at any time of year, but the main breeding season is during the north-west monsoon. The adult leaves the breeding grounds at dawn to feed at sea. It flies close to the surface, gliding on stiff wings mirroring the contours of the ocean. At dusk it returns, and will regurgitate fish for its single chick to eat.

A chick may go hungry for one week or more, but when its parents return it puts on a lot of fat: at nearly three months old, it can weigh twice as much as its parents. At this stage, the parent birds abandon it and, after losing weight, the chick emerges and heads for the open sea — where it may remain for several years before its next landfall.

The fat chicks were taken for food in large numbers in the past, and are still exploited to an extent today.

*Illustrated on following page*

## AUDUBON'S SHEARWATER (Riga)
*Puffinus lherminieri*

This shearwater is commonly seen on sea passages. The largest colony is on Aride with about 40,000 pairs; smaller colonies breed on Cousin, the Amirantes and the Aldabra group. Rafts of up to 10,000 or more birds can be seen offshore near Aride during March and April.

It breeds in burrows but may also use gaps between boulders and other sheltered sites. It may breed at any time of year, but mainly from around January to May. It spends the day at sea; returning after dark with eerie cries.

It is much smaller than the Wedge-tailed Shearwater, and is black above, white below. It feeds its chick until it is heavier than the parent, and abandons the chick so that after about one week it is forced to go out in search of its own food.

Like other shearwaters, it produces large amounts of oil in the gut, which it regurgitates. Sometimes this is done in defence, the oil being directed at intruders to the burrow.

Built for flight and life on the ocean, its legs are placed far back, for swimming, but are inefficient on land. The plumage is dense and waterproof.

*Illustrated on previous page*

## RED-TAILED TROPICBIRD (Payanke Lake Rouz)
*Phaethon rubricauda*

Aride Island, the most northerly Indian Ocean outpost of Seychelles' two tropicbirds, is the only home in the granitic islands for this rarity. The first definite record here was not until 1976 — and not until 1987 was there evidence of more than one nesting pair. Today there may be six to ten pairs. It is much more common on Aldabra where up to 2,000 pairs breed, and it may breed on other raised limestone islands of the Aldabra group.

With a plumper body, proportionately wider wings, and slower wing beats it is not as graceful as the White-tailed Tropicbird. The white body may become flushed with pink during the breeding season. The red tail streamers are thinner and more wire-like than the white feathers of its cousin.

Frequently found in mid-ocean it appears to be much more of an ocean wanderer than other tropicbirds. Otherwise, like other tropicbirds, it is a ground nester, breeding annually, though not always in the same month.

It was once more common and more extensive in its range. Major Stirling, shipwrecked on Astove in August 1836, 'discovered many tropic birds under the bushes; they are of a satiny white, with one long red feather in the tail, some of the other feathers being also slightly tinged with red, sometimes with black'. Sadly future visitors took no further note of these beautiful birds and none have been recorded on Astove since Major Stirling's enforced visit. At least on Aride and Aldabra they are now protected and hopefully will flourish.

*Illustrated on following page*

83

## WHITE-TAILED TROPICBIRD (Payanke)
*Phaethon lepturus*

Two of the world's three species of tropicbird breed in Seychelles. This is by far the more common of the two, with major colonies of up to 2,500 pairs on Aride and 1,000 pairs on Cousin. Smaller populations breed on many of the other granitic islands and on islets within Aldabra Atoll. It also occurs, but much less commonly, in the Amirantes.

The white tail streamers give the bird its Creole name, *payanke*, meaning 'straw-in-tail'. It is the smallest and most elegant of all tropicbirds, with distinctive black markings on the white wings. Young birds are white, barred with greyish black, and lack tail streamers.

A single egg is laid on the ground in the shelter of a boulder or tree stump. It is incubated for about forty days. Fledging takes up to three months and — like shearwaters — a chick puts on a large fat reserve until its weight exceeds that of its parents. At this stage it is abandoned and loses weight rapidly until the threat of starvation forces it to fend for itself.

It breeds year-round, and individual pairs have a nine-month breeding cycle. It plunge dives to catch prey, thought to be mainly flying fish and squid.

The tropicbird is most closely related to the gannet. They are also known as a 'bosunbirds' due to the tail's resemblance to a bosun's spike, and the shrill call to the sound of a bosun's whistle.

The world's third species of tropicbird, the Red-billed Tropicbird, has also been seen in Seychelles' waters, though very rarely. The Christmas Island sub-species of the White-tailed Tropicbird, with a golden yellow wash to the white plumage, has also been seen on occasion.

*Illustrated on previous page*

## RED-FOOTED BOOBY (Fou bet)
*Sula sula*

Up to 7,000 pairs of the Red-footed Booby breed on Aldabra, mainly in mangroves around the inner northern perimeter of the atoll. Cosmoledo also has a fairly large colony and a smaller number breed on Farquhar. It is seen fairly regularly in the granitic islands, especially on Aride.

Generally white, the adults have large sky-blue bills and a yellowish wash on the crown and hindneck. There is a bare patch of skin around the eyes — but its most distinctive characteristic is its huge, bright red feet. Juveniles are dull brown, and some adults also retain this all-brown plumage. With the exception of the brown phase adult, it has a white tail. All other species of booby have dark tails.

One egg is laid, and the huge fat fluffy chick soon achieves the same size as its parents. On Aldabra it nests contentedly alongside the frigatebird. At sea, however, the frigatebird continually harasses it, forcing it to regurgitate its catch.

The word booby comes from the Spanish *bobo*, meaning clown, and the Creole name of *fou*, meaning crazy, is a similar reference to its comical appearance.

*Illustrated on following page*

## MASKED BOOBY (Fou mask, Fou zenero)
*Sula dactylatra*

Also known as the Blue-faced or White Booby, this booby breeds on Cosmoledo, Farquhar, Boudeuse and Étoile. It used to be more widespread at one time, including a large colony on Bird Island, which survived until the 1930s. Being a ground nester, the spread of coconut plantations and the introduction of predators doomed it.

It is similar in appearance to the Red-footed Booby, but has dark brown feet and a 'masked' blackish face. In flight, the trailing edge of the wing is black for its entire length. Juvenile birds are dull brown and white below, with a white collar distinguishing it from all other boobies.

Breeding appears to be fairly widespread throughout the year, but generally occurs during the south-east monsoon.

Boobies have been taken for food in the past — and still are on occasion. They have also been reduced in numbers by other activities such as guano mining, which eliminated both the Masked Booby and Abbot's Booby from Assumption. The latter is now extinct in Seychelles, breeding only on Christmas Island in the Indian Ocean.

*Illustrated on previous page*

## BROWN BOOBY (Fou kapisen)
*Sula leucogaster*

Probably the most common and widespread booby in the world, the Brown Booby is the least common in Seychelles of those known to occur. It still breeds in small numbers on Desnoeufs and possibly elsewhere, but it is a rare sight in the granitic islands.

The adult is dark chocolate brown on the upperparts, head and edges of the wing; the breast and centre of the underwing being white. It may be confused with the juvenile Masked Booby, which is paler brown and has a white upper breast and collar.

The juvenile is similar to the adult, but with dull brown upperparts and the white underparts mottled with brown.

It will perch in trees, but like the Masked Booby, nests only on the ground. Small groups of Brown Boobies will fly at low altitudes — making low-level plunge dives into the sea to snatch flying fish, squid and other food close to the surface.

The Creole name refers to the likeness of the bird's plumage to the habit on a Capuchin monk.

*Illustrated on following page*

## GREAT FRIGATEBIRD (Fregat)
*Fregata minor*

About 1,500 pairs of these fantastic, primitive birds — unable to walk or swim — make Aldabra Atoll their second-largest home on earth. Immature and non-breeding birds may also be seen in the granitic islands, especially Aride.

The adult male has a scarlet throat patch which it can inflate like a balloon in courtship rituals. The female is black above and white below — including the chin. The white underside of the immature bird is entirely confined to the chest.

A pirate of the air, much of its food is taken by chasing boobies, tropicbirds and terns, forcing them to drop or disgorge their catch, but some is caught from close to the ocean surface. It will also take baby turtles as they run from their nest to the sea, or steal unguarded eggs or chicks from the colonies of other birds.

The Great Frigatebird soars above its colony or roosting site with barely a wingbeat, and uses its tail as a rudder to achieve incredible, breathtaking aerial agility. It nests in the mangroves of Aldabra, where it is a good neighbour with the boobies on which it preys.

*Illustrated on previous page*

## LESSER FRIGATEBIRD (Fregat)
*Fregata ariel*

Like the Great Frigatebird, the Lesser Frigatebird breeds only in the Aldabra group, where about 5,000 pairs nest. These ocean wanderers are frequently seen in the granitic Seychelles, but in smaller numbers. On Aride Island, it has been estimated that of about 2,000 roosting frigatebirds, up to seven per cent are Lesser Frigatebirds.

The adult male also has an inflatable throat patch, but unlike the Great Frigatebird is wholly black except for a white flank patch and spurs on the underwings. The female has a black chin and throat, while the immature is usually separable by white spurs extending from the chest onto the underwing. As the name suggests, it is indeed smaller, but the difference is not very obvious in the field.

The Lesser Frigatebird breeds at Aldabra during the south-east monsoon from April to October in mangroves along the northern lagoon shore. It may have nested in the Amirantes, on Bird and Aride islands at one time, but has long since disappeared other than as non-breeding birds.

*Illustrated on following page*

95

## LESSER CRESTED TERN
*Sterna bengalensis*

It is not certain if the Lesser Crested Tern breeds in Seychelles, although it is fairly common in the Aldabra group and is frequently seen in the Amirantes. It is a very rare visitor to the granitic islands.

Though sometimes confused with the Crested Tern, it is smaller and more delicately built, with an orange bill that is darker in the juvenile and non-breeding adult. In breeding plumage, the black cap extends to the base of the bill.

## CRESTED TERN (Golan Sardin)
*Sterna bergii*

An uncommon visitor to the granite islands, this large tern still breeds on Aldabra (with about 50 pairs), some islands in the Amirantes and possibly other coralline islands.

With grey upperparts, white underparts and a black cap, it is much larger and heavier than the Lesser Crested Tern and retains a white forehead in breeding plumage. The bright yellow bill of the breeding adult turns darker, blackish towards the tip outside the breeding seasons, while the crown and lores are white, retaining a black nape and black streak through the eye. Juveniles resemble non-breeding adults with the feathers of the upperparts tipped with dark brown. The large body, heavy drooping bill and large scythe-like wings are good field characteristics for all birds.

*Illustrated on previous page*

## ROSEATE TERN (Dyanman)
*Sterna dougallii*

Widespread from Europe to Australasia, this bird has been in serious decline throughout its range. It has vanished in recent times from four of Seychelles' granitic islands, leaving just the globally important colony on Aride Island, where 1,000 to 1,500 pairs breed during the south-east monsoon. It may also still breed on some of the outer islands.

The Roseate Tern arrives at the breeding grounds in late April. Its bill is black at this time, but rapidly changes to red, and reverts to black again at the end of the nesting season in late August. The breeding bird also has a rosy tinge to the breast.

Unlike the noddy, the Roseate Tern plunge dives from a height of three to five metres (ten to sixteen feet) to snatch small fish from the sea.

The Indian Ocean race was once placed in a separate subspecies, *arideensis* (after Aride Island). Taxonomy is somewhat confused and the race in Seychelles may be included in *bangsi*, also found in the western Pacific.

*Illustrated on following page*

**BRIDLED TERN** (Fansen)
*Sterna anaethetus*

A few hundred pairs of Bridled Terns breed on Aride, Cousin, Récif and the Amirantes. Only on Aride are recent accurate population assessments available, placing it between 1,100 and 1,500 pairs.

Similar in appearance to the Sooty Tern at first glance, the Bridled Tern has a black band through the eye and a narrow white forehead patch stretching behind the eye — giving it a 'bridled' appearance. The upperparts are brownish grey, compared with the black of the Sooty Tern, giving it its other name — Brown Winged Tern — and the back is separated from the black cap by a grey collar.

Unique among the birds of Seychelles, the Bridled Tern breeds in an eight-month cycle. Tropical seabirds are not restricted to a clearly defined summer breeding season and there may be advantages in not 'putting all your eggs in one monsoon', as seasonal and climatic changes can cause breeding failure in one season or another. More study is needed to ascertain breeding success, competition and the diets in different seasons.

*Illustrated on previous page*

## SOOTY TERN (Golet)
*Sterna fuscata*

The most numerous seabird of the Indian Ocean, the Sooty Tern breeds in dense colonies on Desnoeufs, Bird and Aride islands. It formerly bred on Cousin, Frégate, Récif, and Île Sèche, Île Aux Vaches, and Mamelles, but was wiped out by excessive egg collecting, and Aride is now the species' only non-coralline home in the world, except for a small colony on L'Ilot Frégate.

Up to two million pairs breed on the largest colony of Desnoeufs, and about one-quarter that number on Bird. The Aride colony has steadily grown from about 50,000 pairs when the island was established as a reserve in 1973, to about 300,000 pairs today.

Breeding takes place during the south-east monsoon, when they call excitedly 'wideawake' to each other, giving them their other name of 'Wideawake Tern'.

Laying begins in early June and is highly synchronous; almost all the eggs in a colony being laid within a two-week period.

Outside the breeding season, the Sooty Tern is the perfect bird of the sea: it traverses the oceans, hundreds of miles from land, eating and sleeping on the wing until it returns to breed once again. A young bird spends its first five years or so of life out on the oceans.

*Illustrated on following page*

## LESSER NODDY (Kelek, Kordonnyen)
*Anous tenuirostris*

This Indian Ocean speciality has its 'world headquarters' on Aride Island, where up to 200,000 pairs breed. Cousin is probably the world's number two colony. The Aride population has exploded from less than ten per cent of this figure in 1955, mainly due to the regeneration of the mapou forest, which provides nest sites and soft, malleable leaves ideal for nesting material. At one time, mapou was cut in the mistaken belief that the tiny number of birds caught in the sticky seeds posed a threat to the species.

The Lesser Noddy is more streamlined than the Brown Noddy, with a longer, finer bill and a paler crown, which merges evenly with the upperparts. From a distance it appears blackish, whereas the Brown Noddy is more obviously brown.

Before egg laying, the birds gather on the beach at dawn in huge numbers and consume coral fragments as a source of calcium. The eggs are laid in May or June, depending on food availability. Young birds roost around the islands into December, and the adults begin to return around early March.

*Illustrated on previous page*

## BROWN NODDY (Makwa)
*Anous stolidus*

Despite the species' other name — Common Noddy — the Brown Noddy is far less common in Seychelles than the Lesser Noddy. Aride has probably the largest population in the granitic islands with up to 20,000 pairs, while smaller numbers breed on Frégate, Cousin, Mamelles, Récif, and Île Sèche. It also breeds on Bird, Aldabra, and the Amirantes.

A noddy rarely dives below the surface, but feeds on shoals of small fish driven to shallow depths by predatory fish. Fishermen will head towards a group of noddies to search for tuna, bonito, and other game fish.

The noddy differs from all other terns in that it has a wedge-shaped tail — the outer tail feathers becoming progressively shorter. The Brown Noddy may be distinguished from the Lesser Noddy by its relatively stocky appearance, brownish plumage, and more sharply demarcated whitish crown.

The Brown Noddy nests in coconut trees and among granite boulders, unlike the Lesser Noddy which favours mapou woodland. It breeds principally during the south-east monsoon from April to August, but has a secondary season in some sites during the north-west monsoon.

*Illustrated on following page*

## FAIRY TERN (Golan Blan)
*Gygis alba*

The symbol of Air Seychelles, the Fairy Tern is probably the most beautiful of all the islands' seabirds. The graceful flight, the translucence of its wings, the beauty of its pure white plumage and midnight-blue bill, its tameness and eccentric breeding habits endear it to all. Once common, numbers are said to have been decimated by introduced Barn Owls, though rats may have been a bigger problem.

It nests year-round, though there is a peak from January to April. Rough estimates suggest the biggest total population is on Aride with 15,000 to 20,000 pairs, of which up to 6,000 may be present at any one time. Cousin also has a substantial population (perhaps 10,000 pairs), with smaller numbers in the Amirantes islands, Bird and Aldabra.

This elegant white tern lays a single, slightly spherical egg on a bare branch. A newly hatched chick possesses almost fully developed feet to enable it to perch on its precarious home for up to two months before fledging. Many fail, and a high wind can produce a feast for the skinks lurking below the nesting sites.

*Illustrated on previous page*

# 4. MIGRANTS

## NORTHERN ROLLER
*Coracius garrulus*

The Northern or European Roller breeds in warm lowland regions from Spain to Siberia, migrating to southern and eastern Africa for the northern winter. Several million winter in Kenya each year, and a few occasionally stray as far east as Seychelles.

Northern Rollers are brightly coloured birds with a pale blue-green head and underparts and rufous brown back. In flight, the wing feathers show jet black above, brilliant deep blue below, with pale blue patches on the upper wing.

Northern Rollers have frequently been seen on Bird Island, though they only remain for a few days, presumably due to lack of the insects on which they feed. They are frequent visitors to the Aldabra group and have also been seen in the granitics where birds have sometimes settled for weeks or even months. They may set up a feeding station on a telegraph pole or tree. From here they scan the ground for insects, swooping down on their prey.

*Illustrated on following page*

**CRAB PLOVER** (Kavalye)
*Dromas ardeola*

This unique and fascinating bird, the only one in its genus, is a regular visitor to Seychelles. A few birds may turn up at any time of year, but it is most frequently encountered from October to March. Less common in the granitic islands, flocks of hundreds of birds may be seen at Aldabra.

It has a striking black-and-white plumage and a distinctive heavy, black, dagger-shaped bill. The long grey legs project beyond the short tail in flight, and the wings appear long and pointed. Young birds show less contrast between black and white, and have light grey upperparts.

Breeding only in the gulfs of Oman and Aden and in the Red Sea in dense colonies, it is the only wader to nest in a burrow. It excavates its own burrow, more than a metre (three feet) long. The burrow shelves, ending in a chamber where it lays a large, white egg — one of the largest eggs in relation to the size of the bird of any species.

Crabs, worms and molluscs are its main prey. It chases crabs by advancing at a rapid sprint. The huge bill makes short work of the crab's shell.

*Illustrated on previous page*

## GREY PLOVER
*Pluvialis squatarola*

One of the most common northern winter visitors to Seychelles, the Grey Plover is the largest of the plovers outside of the *vanellus* group, and is the only plover to commonly occur the world over.

Outside the breeding season it is plain grey below, with upperparts darker; speckled white.

The Pacific Golden Plover is the only other *pluvialis* plover to commonly winter in Seychelles. It may lose its golden colour altogether, but the dark ear-covert patch, and — in flight — the white underwing with black 'armpits' of the Grey Plover, are distinctive.

## LESSER SAND PLOVER
*Charadrius mongolus*

A regular winter visitor to Seychelles, the Lesser Sand Plover is often seen in association with other waders, including the very similar Greater Sand Plover.

In winter plumage, the adult is smallish, short-legged and shorter billed than the Greater Sand Plover. There are patches on the breast which sometimes may join in a thin band.

It has a rounded head, similar to a Kentish Plover, from which it is distinguished by the lack of a white collar.

*Illustrated on following page*

Opposite top: Grey Plover
Opposite: Lesser Sand Plover
Above: Sanderling
Right: Curlew Sandpiper

## SANDERLING
*Calidris alba*

Typically found as a northern winter visitor to Seychelles, the Sanderling can be seen on sandy beaches actively chasing up and down the shore where the waves are breaking, probing in the wet sand for food.

It is the palest bird of its genus, pearl-grey above white below, with a dark patch often evident on the top outer edge of the wing.

## CURLEW SANDPIPER
*Calidris ferruginea*

The most common sandpiper to winter in Seychelles, the Curlew Sandpiper can frequently be seen on sheltered sandy beaches or mudflats.

Outside its breeding season, it is plain grey-brown above and white below, with a little grey-brown on the sides. It is large for a sandpiper, with a longish, curved black bill and long black legs. It breeds around the Siberian Arctic Ocean.

Other sandpipers frequently seen in Seychelles include the Common Sandpiper, Terek Sandpiper and various stints.

*Illustrated on previous page*

## WHIMBREL (Korbizo)
*Numenius phaeopus*

The only curlew to breed all around the entire circumference of northern latitudes, the Whimbrel also has the widest non-breeding range and is one of the more common northern winter visitors.

Its upperparts are dark brown and speckled, with paler underparts, streaked with dark markings on the sides and chest. It has a prominent white stripe through the eye, a black crown stripe, and a long, decurved bill.

The larger, paler Curlew — with its longer decurved bill — is also a frequent, but less common, winter visitor to Seychelles.

## GREENSHANK
*Tringa nebularia*

One of the most common northern winter visitors, the Greenshank's ringing three or four-syllable flight call is a characteristic sound to be heard on the mudflats around Victoria.

Its upperparts are pale grey and white below, with streaks on the neck and breast. In flight, the wings appear quite dark and a white V-shape extends from the tail up the back. The legs are dull olive-green.

It may be confused with the similar, more delicately proportioned Marsh Sandpiper, which is another winter visitor to Seychelles, though much less common.

*Illustrated on following page*

**117**

118

*Opposite top: Whimbrel*
*Opposite: Greenshank*

## WOOD SANDPIPER
*Tringa glareola*

One of the most abundant and widespread of its genus, the Wood Sandpiper is also one of the strongest migrants. Unlike most other waders, it prefers inland waters to the intertidal zone. A few reach Seychelles each year, where they frequent small or temporary pools.

It may be confused with the Green Sandpiper, which also occasionally reaches Seychelles, but the Wood Sandpiper is paler underneath and browner on the back. Young birds have distinctly spotted backs.

*Illustrated on previous page*

## TURNSTONE (Bezros)
*Arenaria interpres*

This small, stocky wader is one of the most common northern winter visitors to Seychelles, occurring throughout the islands. A few birds remain for the summer, but the majority migrate to the breeding grounds on the coasts of the Arctic Ocean and the lowland plains of northern Siberia.

Remarkably, one Turnstone ringed on Cousin was recovered two years later by a British ornithologist working near the Aral Sea, and turned up again on La Digue another two years on, just twenty kilometres (twelve miles) from where it was ringed. It appeared this individual was no wind-blown vagrant, but deliberately pinpointed the granitic Seychelles as its winter retreat.

The non-breeding plumage, almost always characteristic of Seychelles birds, is dull brown above, feathers fringed with buffish white, white below, head dark and a slate-grey breast band. Occasionally, traces of chestnut on the upperparts indicate a bird changing between breeding and non-breeding plumages.

*Illustrated on following page*

## BROAD-BILLED ROLLER (Katiti Madagaskar)
*Eurystomus glaucurus*

This stocky roller breeds in Madagascar and sub-Saharan Africa. Malagasy birds migrate to East Africa during the southern winter, and it is almost certainly these birds that turn up in Seychelles — especially in the Aldabra group, where they are regularly seen.

The Broad-billed Roller is a stout, darkish bird, with a rufous head and upperparts except for the sky-blue rump and tail, and navy blue trailing edge to the wings. It has a heavy, bright yellow bill.

It can only be confused with the Madagascar Kestrel, and indeed, this is the Creole name for the bird.

*Illustrated on previous page*

---

## Photographs

---

# INDEX

| | Text Page | Illustration Page |
|---|---|---|